THE BIRTH PARTNER

THE
BIRTH
PARTNER

Everything
You Need to Know
to Help a Woman
through Childbirth

Penny Simkin, P.T.

THE HARVARD COMMON PRESS
Harvard and Boston, Massachusetts

The Harvard Common Press
535 Albany Street
Boston, Massachusetts 02118

Printed in the United States of America

Library of Congress Cataloging-in-Publication Data

Simkin, Penny, 1938–
   The birth partner : everything you need to know to help a woman
through childbirth / Penny Simkin.
      p.   cm.
   Includes index.
   ISBN 1-55832-011-3 : $16.95 — ISBN 1-55832-010-5 (pbk.) : $8.95
   1. Pregnancy—Popular works.   2. Childbirth—Popular works.
I. Title.
RG525.S5829   1989
618.4—dc19

Photographs by Artemis
Drawings by Childbirth Graphics
Cover design by Jackie Schuman
Text design by Linda Ziedrich

10 9 8 7 6 5 4 3 2 1

To my son, Andy, the birth partner closest to my heart; his wife, Bess, who really taught him how to be a birth partner; and their sons, Freddy and Charley, whose births I was privileged to attend. They were my main inspiration for writing this book.

CONTENTS

ACKNOWLEDGMENTS

I have had my share of support through the process of writing this book. I want to thank Marge Mansfield, Licensed Midwife; Janet Whalley, BSN; Paul Norlen; Karin Paulsen; and Andy and Bess Simkin for reading and commenting on portions of the manuscript. Bess and Andy, my daughter-in-law and son, provided me with a rare opportunity to explore their experiences with birth in minute detail. Leslie Jordan, Laurie Douglas, and Kim Burg, young mothers from my childbirth class, caught me in a "teachable moment" and provided me with wonderful insights into their feelings during childbirth. Leslie named the "Take-Charge Routine" when I was groping for an appropriate term.

Wanda Boe, my secretary, went far beyond the call of duty in preparing the manuscript. Maureen Lucier and Linda Ziedrich, my editors, were extremely patient and helpful.

Finally, my husband, Peter, and my children have been sympathetic and accepting of my preoccupation with this book over the past months. We are all looking forward to spending more time together.

Introduction

Congratulations! You are to be a birth partner. You have the privilege and responsibility of accompanying a woman through one of the truly unforgettable events of her life—the birth of her baby. If it is also your baby, this birth is even more significant to you. If you love the woman, as her husband, lover, mother, friend, or other loved one, this birth and the woman's experience of it mean a great deal to you. Even if you hardly know the woman—if you are, for example, a nurse, a childbirth educator, a professional labor support person, or a student of nursing, midwifery, or medicine—you still recognize how important this birth and baby are to her, and you want to help her to have a positive and gratifying experience.

A woman never forgets her experiences in giving birth. And she will never forget you and how you helped her.

Although I have written this book *to* you, I have written it *for* her. My wishes for every pregnant woman are that she and her baby remain healthy, and that she find fulfillment and gratification as she gives birth. A team of people helps her to give birth safely and with satisfaction: her caregivers (midwife, physician, or both), one or more nurses, and her birth partner(s). Your main role as her birth partner is to help her have the kind of birth she desires. And the purpose of this book is to help you help her. Having given birth myself to four children, having been present at the birth of my two grandsons, having provided labor support for numerous women, having spent more than twenty years teaching and learning from thousands of women and their partners, I am ready to share what I know with you.

In helping to create a fulfilling memory for your partner, you do the same for yourself. Helping a woman through childbirth and witnessing the birth of a baby rank among the high points of life.

The Language of Childbirth

As you will soon discover, there are many unfamiliar concepts and a whole new language related to pregnancy and birth. It may seem confusing at first, but you will want to understand these terms in order to communicate with nurses, caregivers (midwives and doctors), and others who are knowledgeable about the subject. To help you, I have used familiar descriptive words along with the terms actually used in most books and by professionals.

To assist you further, the index is arranged so that the page number where a term is first defined is set in boldface italic type, so you can look it up if you are uncertain about its meaning. For example, to learn the meaning of *dilation of cervix*, look it up in the index, where it appears as follows:

Dilation of cervix, *40*, 41, 42, 49, 50, 57

On page *40*, you will find *dilation of cervix* defined or explained. On the other pages you will find further discussion of the subject.

As you become familiar with the new language, you will become more comfortable with it.

How to Use This Book

The Birth Partner is intended to be useful both as a guide to prepare you in advance for your role as birth partner and also as a quick reference during labor. Try to read the entire book before the mother goes into labor. Then, if there is time, you may want to review parts of it during labor.

But there may also be times during labor when you need immediate help and want to find something quickly in this book. I have tried to anticipate which information you may need on the spot and have indicated those sections by darkening the page edges. Fan the pages of the book and find those with dark edges. Their titles are listed right on the edge for quick reference. These sections are—

Part One

BEFORE
THE BIRTH

*T*HE BIRTH PARTNER'S ROLE IDEALLY BEGINS BEFORE THE mother is actually in labor. During the last few weeks of her pregnancy, you can learn about labor, encourage her to continue good health habits, and help her with last-minute preparations for the baby and for labor itself.

1
The Last Few Weeks of Pregnancy

*E*arly in pregnancy, it seems that nine months is forever and that there is plenty of time to do everything that has to be done. It is all too easy, especially for busy people, to postpone "getting into" the pregnancy. Now, suddenly, the baby is almost due. Time has flown by. As the mother's birth partner, you realize she is counting on you to help her through childbirth. Do you feel ready? Can you help her? What do you know about labor? Do you know what to do when? What should you do now to get ready for the baby?

It is not too late to learn and do what needs to be done. But you had better start right away—a few weeks before the due date is truly the "last minute," especially since many babies arrive early. This first chapter is basically a checklist of things you should do before labor starts, to help ensure that you will work well with the mother during the labor and birth. Also included are suggestions about how you can help prepare beforehand for the baby's arrival.

Getting Ready for Labor

If you haven't already done the things described in the following pages, try to get them done a few weeks before the due date, or at least before labor starts.

Visit the Mother's Caregiver (Doctor or Midwife)

If you have not yet met the mother's caregiver, this visit may be more important than you think for both the caregiver and yourselves! Even a brief meeting helps establish you to the caregiver as an important person in the mother's life. It also provides you with an opportunity to ask your own questions and to play a more active role. You will feel more as if you belong at the birth if you have had a chance to meet the mother's caregiver in advance.

Visit the Hospital

If possible, take a tour of the hospital maternity area—birthing rooms, nursery, and postpartum rooms. At the very least, figure out your route to the hospital, how long it takes to get there, and which entrances to use during the day and at night (you usually use the main entrance during the day and the emergency entrance at night). If the mother is planning a home birth, be sure to visit the backup hospital so that you won't be confused if a transfer to the hospital becomes necessary.

Preregister at the Hospital

Preregistering involves obtaining, reading, and signing preadmission forms and a medical consent form. By registering in advance, you save time and avoid confusion when the mother is in labor.

Be Sure You Can Always Be Reached by Phone

If necessary, rent a beeper (check the Yellow Pages under "paging systems"). If your job takes you far away, plan to have someone else available when you are not.

Review What You Learned in Childbirth Classes

If you have taken classes, review your handouts and notes. Gather those materials that you might want to refer to during labor—lists, suggestions, questionnaires, information about your hospital's services.

Gather the Necessary Supplies

What do you pack for the hospital? What do you need for a home birth? The following lists should help.

Supplies to Take to the Hospital. Try to pack as many of these things in advance as possible.

- *For the mother's use during labor—*
  - Oil or cornstarch for massage (unscented is best)
  - Lip balm
  - Toothbrush
  - Her own gown and robe if she prefers them to hospital clothes
  - Rolling pin, camper's ice, or plastic, teardrop-shaped detergent bottle filled with water and frozen (choose one that has no spout in the cap so it will not leak as the ice melts)—for pressure and cold on low back
  - Warm socks and slippers
  - Tapes of favorite relaxing music, and tape player
  - Personal focal point (a picture, flowers, a figurine) for her to focus on during contractions
  - Favorite juice, popsicles, or electrolyte-balanced beverage (such as Gatorade) in a cooler
- *For the birth partner's use—*
  - Copy of the Birth Plan (see page 20)
  - Watch with second hand
  - Grooming supplies (toothbrush, breath freshener, deodorant, shaver)
  - Food for snacks, such as sandwiches, fruit, cheese and crackers, beverages (consider beforehand what they will do to your breath)
  - Sweater
  - Change of clothes
  - Swimsuit so you can accompany the mother in the shower
  - Paper and pencil
  - This book
  - Other reading materials, or handwork, for slow times when the mother does not need your help
  - Phone numbers of people to call during or after labor
  - Change or credit card for pay phone, if needed
  - Camera (still or video), film or videotape, batteries, audio tape and recorder
- *For the mother's use during the postpartum period—*
  - Gowns that open in front for breastfeeding, unless she prefers hospital gowns
  - Robe and slippers
  - Cosmetics, toilet articles

Tasty snack foods, such as fruit, nuts, cheese and crackers—her favorite treats

Nursing bras

Reading and writing materials, address book, birth announcements

Money for incidentals

Going-home clothing

- *For the baby—*

  Clothing: diapers and pins, waterproof pants, undershirt, gown or stretch suit, receiving blanket, outer clothing (hat, warm clothing), crib-size blanket

  Car seat

- *For the trip to the hospital—*

  A full tank of gas

  A blanket and pillow in the car

Supplies for Home Birth. Look over the preceding lists for ideas about what to have at home. In addition, consider the following:

- *Birthing supplies* (caregivers usually provide a list), such as—

  Disposable waterproof underpads (Chux pads)

  Sterile four-by-four-inch gauze pads

  K-Y jelly

  Bulb syringe

  Cord clamps

  Squeeze bottle to cleanse perineum

  Long, hospital-sized sanitary napkins

  Sanitary belt

  Rubber gloves

  Betadine (a cleansing solution)

  Thermometer

  Hat for the baby

  Basin for the placenta

  Washcloths and hand towels

  Flexible straws

  Trash bags

  Waterproof mattress cover

  Wet, folded washcloths placed in plastic bags and frozen

  Food for caregivers and birthing team during labor

  Food and drink for birth celebration

  A map to your home, for the caregiver

Other last-minute preparations: turn up the water heater, clean and organize the house, make the bed with fresh linens, and prepare the baby's area. In case of transfer to a hospital, know the way to the back-up hospital, be sure your car's gas tank is full, and include in the Birth Plan the mother's preferences in case of transfer (see "Review the Mother's Birth Plan," page 20).

Encourage the Mother to Drink Plenty of Fluids

The mother should drink at least two quarts of liquid a day—water, fruit juices, clear soups. This helps support her increased fluid needs during pregnancy.

Help Her Switch to a High-Carbohydrate Diet

Just as an endurance athlete benefits from "carbo-loading" for a few days before an athletic event, a pregnant woman may benefit from a high-carbohydrate (high-starch) diet at the end of pregnancy in preparation for her "event"—labor.

Benefits of a High-Carbohydrate Diet. A diet high in starchy foods has been shown to increase the amount of glycogen stored in muscle. During muscular exertion, the glycogen is converted to glucose, the muscle's energy source. If the body's glycogen stores are depleted, then fat is converted into glycogen. Fat conversion, however, does not work as well as glycogen conversion. As fat is used to provide energy, byproducts called ketone bodies accumulate in the blood, causing ketosis, a condition that can slow labor or, if the buildup is great, even cause fetal distress. If a laboring woman develops ketosis, intravenous fluids containing dextrose (sugar) may be given to provide energy and thus correct the ketosis. A high-carbohydrate diet late in pregnancy may provide enough glycogen to prevent ketosis.

Foods She Should Eat. During the last few days of pregnancy, the mother should shift toward carbohydrates as her major source of calories. The following foods help build glycogen stores in muscle: bread, crackers, cereal, corn, pasta, potatoes, rice, and fresh fruit. Protein and fat should make up a smaller proportion of her diet than carbohydrates. Small amounts of milk or cheese, meat, fish, tofu, lentils, and very small amounts of butter, margarine, and oil can be added to make the starchy foods more tasty. In addition, she should not ignore fresh vegetables.

A similar diet might benefit you as well; your support role in labor can also be physically demanding.

In early labor, and especially in the slow-to-start labor (page 97), the mother should drink plenty of water, fruit juice, and electrolyte-balanced "athletes' drinks" like Gatorade, ERG, and others. In addition, she should eat easily digested, high-carbohydrate, starchy foods. These can help prevent undue fatigue.

Encourage Her to Exercise

Regular exercise, like walking or swimming, will help to maintain the mother's general fitness. In addition, a few special exercises are particularly helpful during late pregnancy and labor. These are squatting, the pelvic rock on hands and knees, and the Kegel (pelvic-floor contraction) exercise. Encourage the mother to do these every day.

Squatting. Squatting may be very useful in helping the baby come down during the birthing stage (see page 60), but, because it is not a customary position for Westerners, the mother may need to get used to it before labor begins.

She should stand with her feet wide enough apart that she can keep her heels on the floor as she squats. Then she lowers herself into a squatting position. It is not necessary that she have perfect balance. She can hold onto you, the arm of a couch, or doorknobs on either side of a door. She can also rest her back against a wall or against you, if you sit behind her. Once squatting, she should remain in the position (without bouncing) for up to one minute (she might begin with twenty seconds and gradually increase the time). Then she rises to standing. If she does ten squats a day, she will rapidly become accustomed to the position.

If her insteps roll in, she can correct this by placing her heels on books (one to two inches thick). This way she still has her weight on her heels while relieving pressure on her insteps.

A woman should *not* practice squatting if it causes her undue or lasting pain. She should also refrain from this exercise if she has hip, knee, or ankle problems that could be worsened by squatting.

Pelvic Rock on Hands and Knees. During pregnancy, this exercise helps strengthen abdominal muscles, relieve low back pain, improve circulation in the lower half of the body, and position the baby in the OA (occiput anterior) position (page 36). During labor it helps relieve back pain and rotate the baby.

The mother should get down on her hands and knees, and make herself "square"; that is, her thighs and arms should be perpendicular to the floor and her back straight, not sagging. Then she tucks her "tail" under, feeling the tightening of her abdominal muscles and some stretching and arching in her low back. She holds the position for ten seconds, then returns to the original position. (This exercise is easy to do while reading the newspaper!) She repeats this ten times a day.

The Kegel (Pelvic Floor Contraction) Exercise. This is the most important of the three exercises to a woman's lifelong general health, because it strengthens muscles that support the pelvic organs and that are vital to sexual pleasure. During childbirth, good tone in these muscles helps the baby rotate and descend. The mother's ability to relax these muscles in the second stage as she pushes her baby down will greatly assist the birth.

There are two components of the Kegel exercise—toning and bulging.

1. *Pelvic floor toning.* The mother contracts the muscles of her pelvic floor as she might when she is trying to keep from urinating or stopping the flow of urine once it has begun. She can do some quick contractions ("flicks") and hold others for up to ten seconds. She will find that the longer holds are difficult to maintain; these muscle fibers seem to fatigue fairly quickly, even in women with good tone. If the contraction seems to disappear or fade, even when she has not consciously let go, she should simply renew it by tightening again. She lets go after five or ten seconds. She should try not to contract muscles in her legs, buttocks, or abdomen, or to hold her breath while doing the exercise.

She should try to do this exercise fifty to one hundred times a day (the five- to ten-second holds at least twenty times a day). You can remind her to do it while riding in the car or bus, waiting in line, or talking on the telephone.

2. *Pelvic floor bulging.* This exercise is a rehearsal for "letting go" as the baby stretches the vagina and comes out. The mother can help the baby emerge by relaxing her pelvic floor muscles, rather than tensing or tightening them. This is how she should practice:

After doing a five- or ten-second hold, she lets go of the contraction and then consciously bulges her pelvic floor by holding her breath and gently straining as she would to press out the last few drops of urine or a bowel movement. She then teaches herself to bulge her pelvic floor while exhaling. We sometimes call this the "elevator" exercise. The pelvic floor is the elevator. As the mother gradually contracts her muscles, the elevator is going up floor by floor; as she lets go, the elevator is coming down floor by floor; as she bulges, the elevator is going to the basement. She should always conclude the exercise by contracting, then relaxing the pelvic floor. Five to ten of these bulging exercises a day are probably enough to prepare her for the birth.

A woman should do the pelvic floor toning exercise all her life. The bulging exercise is important for only a few weeks before birth.

Use Prenatal Perineal Massage

Regular massage of a woman's perineum (the area between the vagina and the anus) in late pregnancy helps prepare the perineum to stretch adequately during the birth. Prenatal perineal massage can reduce the need for an episiotomy (a surgical incision to enlarge the vagina, done just before the birth); and it may reduce the likelihood that the mother's tissues will lacerate (tear) seriously during birth. Prenatal perineal massage lets the expectant mother experience sensations that are similar to those she will feel as the baby emerges, and it gives her a chance to practice relaxing her perineum as she should during delivery.

Perineal massage has not been thoroughly evaluated scientifically, but the few studies done indicate that it does indeed accomplish these purposes. I advise the pregnant women in my classes to use this massage for four to six weeks before their due date. Frankly, some women find it distasteful and decide not to do it; others find it pleasurable or sexually stimulating, which is a bonus. Most who do it regularly find it very beneficial.

Caution: If vaginitis, a herpes sore, or other vaginal problems exist, perineal massage could worsen or spread the condition and should not be done until the problem goes away.

Instructions for Perineal Massage. Either you or the expectant mother herself can do the massage. These directions are for you. Be sure your fingernails are short. Wash your hands before beginning. If you have rough skin on your fingers, which might scratch her, wear disposable rubber gloves.

The expectant mother should make herself comfortable in a semi-sitting position, with her legs bent and relaxed.

1. Lubricate your fingers well with wheat germ or other vegetable oil or water-soluble jelly. Do not use baby oil, mineral oil, or petroleum jelly, as they tend to dry the tissue; vegetable oils are better

absorbed. To avoid contaminating the oil, do not dip your fingers in the oil; instead, squirt the oil over your fingers.

2. Rub enough oil or jelly into the perineum (area between the vagina and the anus) to allow your fingers to move smoothly over the tissue and lower vaginal wall.

3. Use your index fingers. Start with one and progress to two. Place your fingers well inside the expectant mother's vagina (up to the second knuckle); rotate them in opposite directions upward along the sides and lower border while pulling outward gently. Do this for about three minutes. This movement will stretch the vaginal tissue, the muscles surrounding the vagina, and the skin of the perineum.

4. Finish the massage by rubbing the skin of the perineum between the thumb and forefinger (thumb on the outside, finger on the inside) for about one minute. In the beginning, the tissue feels tight, but with time and repeated massages it relaxes and stretches. The massage takes four or five minutes.

5. Tell the expectant mother to concentrate on relaxing her perineum as she feels the pressure. As she becomes more comfortable with the massage, increase the pressure just enough to make the perineum begin to sting from the stretching. This same stinging sensation will occur as the baby's head is being born.

6. Ask your caregiver or your childbirth educator to answer any questions you may have after trying the massage.

Consider Keeping Track of Fetal Movements

Fetal movement counting is a test of the baby's well-being that can detect a problem in time to prevent serious harm. Although most babies have no problems in the uterus, some do, and a major purpose of maternity care is to prevent, detect, or treat such problems.

Recent research on fetal activity has shown that an active baby is a healthy baby. If a baby is not doing well or is not getting enough oxygen or nourishment from his mother via the placenta, he will slow his movements to conserve energy. There is usually a period of decreasing movement—enough time to act—before the baby is in serious trouble.

The mother can provide an accurate account of fetal movements. This information can help the caregiver decide whether other tests of fetal well-being are necessary or whether to deliver the baby early. The mother is most likely to assess fetal movements correctly if she sets aside a period of time each day and keeps a written record of the number of fetal movements. Such a record is more accurate than the mother's informal impressions, which are influenced by how busy or distracted she is at any particular time.

Some caregivers ask all their pregnant clients to keep a daily or every-other-day record of fetal movements from about the thirty-second week of pregnancy. Others ask only those clients who are at high risk for fetal problems. Many women find fetal movement counting to be fun and interesting. Not only do they gather helpful information, but they enjoy the time spent focusing on their babies. They learn about different types of movements, about their babies' sleep and wake cycles, and about other things. Other women find fetal movement counting makes them worry; they feel they are just waiting for something to go wrong.

If the mother decides to count fetal movements, do it with her, at least some of the time. You can learn a lot about the baby too, and you can also support the mother if she finds it stressful.

There are several ways to do fetal movement counting. The "Count-to-Ten" method, which follows, is simple and can be begun at any time in late pregnancy.

How to Count Fetal Movements. It is most helpful if the mother counts the baby's movements each day, beginning any time after the thirty-second week of pregnancy. (If she skips a day now and then, she should simply resume counting the next day.) It makes sense to begin counting when the baby is awake and active.

She indicates with an *S* on the chart the time she starts counting. A movement may be a short kick or wiggle, or a long, continuous squirming. She waits for a pause in activity and counts it as one movement. The pause may last only a few seconds or, if the baby falls asleep, more than an hour. Hiccups do not count as movements.

When she has counted ten fetal movements, she stops counting, and fills in the box corresponding to the time period during which the tenth movement occurred. For instance, if she starts counting at 9:00 A.M., she places an *S* in the box for that time. If she felt the tenth movement at 12:20 P.M., she fills in the box for 12:30 P.M. If she does not feel ten movements in twelve hours, she should write down the number of movements she has felt, and call her caregiver to report this information. In addition, if she finds the baby seems to be "slowing down"—that is, taking longer and longer over a period of several days to complete ten movements, she should report this finding as well.

FETAL MOVEMENT COUNTING CHART

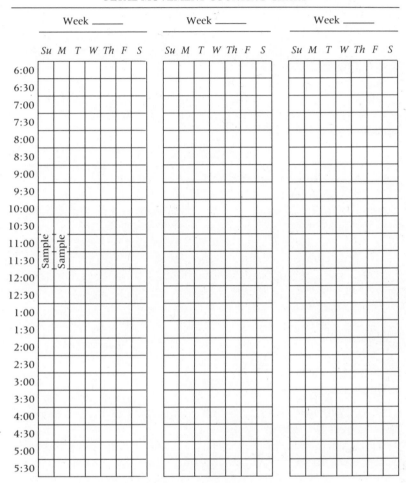

Prepare Other Children for the Birth

Things go more smoothly if siblings are prepared in advance for the arrival of a new brother or sister. It reassures children to know where their mother will be giving birth, where they will be, and who will be with them. And they will surely benefit from being included, as appropriate, in preparations for the new baby.

See "Recommended Resources," for books on the subject of children and birth.

Review the Mother's Birth Plan

So that you will really know how to help her, become familiar with the mother's written Birth Plan. The Birth Plan tells everyone involved in her care what options are important to her, what her priorities are, and how she would like to be cared for. If you are the mother's life partner (lover, husband, father of the baby) as well as her birth partner, the Birth Plan should be written by both of you. If you are not intimately involved with the mother, the Birth Plan should be hers, and you should be very familiar with it.

Although Birth Plans are most useful for births in hospitals, where the nurses (and often the caregivers) do not know the mother, it is useful for everyone, even those planning home births, to think through their priorities and choices. It helps if the two of you go over the plan together with the caregiver. At the least, however, be ready to help the staff follow the mother's plan, and be ready to remind her of some of her prior choices when she is caught up in the intense demands of labor.

Keep a copy of the Birth Plan with you during labor. Use it as a guide, but remember that you both should be flexible and willing to accept changes in the plan if medical circumstances require it.

Discuss with the mother beforehand the following points in the Birth Plan and any other details that seem appropriate.

Introduction to the Birth Plan. The plan might begin with the following information:

- *Personal Information.* What would the mother like the staff to know about her? For example, she might describe strongly held beliefs or preferences, relevant previous experiences with hospitals or health care, fears, or other information that would help the staff get to know her and treat her as a special individual.
- *Message to the Staff.* Would she like to express her appreciation for any support, expertise, and assistance the staff can provide to help her have a safe and satisfying birth experience?

Labor Options. The mother can consider the following options for labor:

- *Birthing room.* Does the mother want to use a birthing room, if available, or conventional labor and delivery rooms?
- *Activity in labor.* Does she want the freedom to walk, change positions, take a bath or shower, or move about in labor to promote

comfort or progress? Or will she be content to remain in bed? (See "Movement and Position Changes," page 76.)

- *Food and drink.* Does she prefer to eat and drink at will, or is she comfortable with having intravenous fluids (page 126) and sucking ice chips?
- *Fetal heart rate monitoring.* How does she feel about continuous electronic monitoring (internal or external), intermittent monitoring, or, instead, having a nurse or caregiver listen with an ultrasound stethoscope or a regular stethoscope? (See "Electronic Fetal Monitoring," page 128.)
- *Pain medications.* Does she plan to use them? Does she want to avoid them? How important is this to her? (See chapter 8, "Medications for Pain during Labor," page 161, including the "Pain Medications Preference Scale," page 163, for important information and pointers.)

Birth Options. The mother can consider the following options for birth:

- *Positions for second (birthing) stage.* Would the mother prefer to be free to move, and to use a variety of positions, or is she content to be semireclining or flat on her back with her legs in footrests or stirrups? (See "Positions for Second Stage," page 77.)
- *Pushing techniques.* Does she prefer to use the spontaneous, non-directed bearing-down technique or the prolonged breathholding and straining of directed pushing? (See "Breathing Patterns for Pushing," page 89.)
- *Episiotomy.* Would she prefer to have an episiotomy, or not? How strongly does she feel about it? Would she rather risk a tear than have an episiotomy? (See "Episiotomy," page 138.)

After-Birth Options. The mother can consider the following options in postpartum care:

- *General preferences.* Are the usual routines for baby care acceptable? Does the mother want the staff to do most of the baby care? Or do the two of you prefer to do it? Do you want to be informed in advance of all procedures involving the baby?
- *Immediate care of the baby.* Do you and the mother have preferences regarding newborn routines (eye care, vitamin K, newborn exam, and so forth)? (See "Common Procedures in Newborn Care," page 197, and "The Next Few Days for the Baby," page 202.)
- *Contact with the baby.* Does the mother want continuous contact

with the baby? How does she feel about the baby's spending time in the nursery? Does she want the baby with her at night as well as during the day? Does she prefer to have the baby for feeding only?

- *Your presence.* Would the mother like you to stay in the hospital with her? Can you bring in a cot and sleep there overnight?
- *Feeding.* Will the baby be breastfed or formula fed? If she is breast-feeding, how does the mother feel about the baby's being given water, sugar water, or formula? Does she want to feed the baby on demand (that is, when the baby expresses hunger), or on a pre-determined schedule? (See "Getting Started with Breastfeeding," page 215.) If the baby is to be formula fed, do the two of you want to do all the feeding yourselves or do you want to have the nurses do some of it?
- *Circumcision.* If the baby is a boy, will he be circumcised or not? (See "Circumcision" in chapter 10, page 203.)
- *Discharge from the hospital.* Does the mother want a short stay—that is, does she want to leave the hospital within twenty-four hours after a vaginal birth—or the usual hospital stay of two to three days (see "Discharge from the Hospital," page 208)?

The Unexpected. The mother should think through the possibility of these difficulties:

- *Difficult labor.* Is the Birth Plan flexible enough to apply even if complications or difficulties arise during labor? If difficulties do arise, does the mother still want to be consulted before procedures are performed, or would she prefer to leave all decisions to the staff?
- *Transfer.* If she develops complications and has to be transferred from a birthing room or home to a hospital labor room, does she have some preferences regarding her care? For example: Does she want you and any other support people to remain with her? Does she want the original Birth Plan to be respected, and does she want to keep whatever options are still possible? Does she want her caregivers to seek her informed consent for all procedures, as long as it is medically safe to do so?
- *Cesarean birth.* Does the mother want you to be present? Would she prefer to be awake? Would she like to see and touch the baby afterwards? What about postoperative sedation? Would she prefer to receive sleep or sedative medications afterwards or to accept early trembling and discomfort in order to remain awake and to hold

and nurse the baby? (See chapter 9, "Cesarean Childbirth," page 181.)

- *Premature or sick infant.* Would the mother prefer to be involved, or have you involved, as much as possible in the care and feeding of the baby, even if the baby is in the special care unit? Does she want explanations of the baby's problems, the procedures to be done, and the decisions that need to be made? Does she want you to accompany the baby to a different hospital if the baby has to be transferred? Does she want to express her colostrum (the "pre-milk" her breasts make during the first two or three days after birth) and her milk to store until the baby can take it?

- *Stillbirth or death of the baby.* Such a tragedy leaves the parents so stunned with grief that it is almost impossible for them to make important decisions. Discuss this possibility together and think about how you and the mother would want the situation handled. Weeks or months after the death of a baby, the things that were done (or not done) at the time will be very important. Consider some or all of the following:

    An opportunity to hold and say good-bye to the baby in private

    A chance to dress the baby

    Mementos—pictures, the baby's clothing or blanket, a lock of hair, hand and footprints

    Help from a counselor or a member of the clergy

    An opportunity to discuss the birth and the baby's problems with the doctor, midwife, and nurses

    An autopsy to determine the cause of death

    A memorial service or funeral—an opportunity for family and friends to acknowledge the baby's life and death and to demonstrate their love, support, and sympathy for the parents

As difficult as it may be to face the possibility that the baby could die, it is wise to think through this situation. I hope you will never need to implement any of the above suggestions. If you do, you will be glad later that you had thought about it ahead of time, when you were calm and able to think clearly.

Personal Choices. Are there other choices that will help make this birth experience more comfortable or memorable for the mother and for you? Consider doing the following:

    Providing her favorite music

    Including others—relatives, friends, interpreter (if needed) or children

Excluding nonessential personnel (for example, students, observers)

Having you assist in delivering the baby's body or cut the cord

Photographing, videotaping, or audiotaping the birth

Using comfort items such as toothbrush, lip balm, cold packs, eyeglasses (if needed), lollipops, ice or fluids, items for backrubs, warm socks, cornstarch or oil for massage, and so forth

Using gentle birth procedures (dim lights, low noise, gentle handling of the baby, warm bath soon after birth to help relax the baby)

Welcoming the baby (with private time together, with music, or with a religious or personal ceremony)

Incorporating culturally significant customs (foods, bathing, contact with baby, and so forth)

Make sure you know the mother's preferences, and be sure they are included in her written Birth Plan.

Preparing for Life with the Baby

Following is a reminder list of some things to try to do before the baby is born. It is much easier to do these things before the birth than afterwards, when time and energy will be more limited. If you are the mother's life partner (husband, lover), you will want to make these preparations together. If not, you might advise her that these need to be done.

Gather the Essential Supplies for the Baby

Is everything ready for the baby? Are the necessary supplies on hand? Use the lists that follow as a guide.

- *Baby equipment*
    Car seat
    Crib, bassinet, or cradle
- *Bedding (minimum requirements)*
    Two or more fitted sheets (pillowcases often fit bassinette mattresses)
    Two square waterproof pads to fit under the baby's diaper area
    Two warm, crib-sized blankets or quilts
    Three receiving blankets
- *Clothing* (Buy baby clothes with room for the baby to grow—no

smaller than ten- to twelve-pound size. Babies usually weigh ten pounds by the time they are one or two months old, if not at birth. Often, the baby will outgrow even six-month-size clothes by the time she is two or three months old.)

Four snap- or tie-front (not pullover) undershirts
Three one-piece coveralls (stretch suits, sleepers)
Three nightgowns
Two sweaters
One hat for indoors the first few days
One hat for outdoors
One warm outfit for outdoors
Two pairs of booties
Four diaper covers (plastic pants or soakers)
At least two to four dozen diapers and a diaper pail, unless the mother has a diaper service
Three pairs of diaper pins or clips
Two baby bath towels
Two washcloths

- *Health supplies*
  Blunt fingernail scissors
  Rectal thermometer
  Cornstarch for powdering diaper area
  Diaper rash ointment
  Baby wipes
  Rubber bulb syringe for nose (The hospital usually provides a long, pointed rubber syringe. Be sure the nurse shows you and the mother how to use it properly, or buy one with a blunt plastic tip, which is better designed for long-term use.)
- *Supplies for Breastfeeding*
  At least two well-fitting nursing bras for the mother
  Nursing pads (commercially available, or she can make her own—six layers of cotton flannel cut to fit inside her bra and sewn together)
  Plain lanolin for treating sore nipples
- *Supplies for formula feeding*
  Supply of formula
  Eight to twelve bottles, nipples, caps
  Large pot for sterilizing bottles
  Tongs, funnel, glass (Pyrex) measuring cup
- *Optional paraphernalia*
  Bumper pads for crib

Mobile (choose one that looks interesting from below, where the baby is)

Infant seat (an infant car seat can double as one of these)

Soft front-carrier—to strap the baby onto you or the mother

Stroller or carriage

Baby swing

Rocking chair

Baby bathtub

Pacifiers (for babies who need to suck a great deal)

Breast pump (if the mother will want to express and store breast milk)

Intercom (if the baby will sleep beyond easy hearing range)

Tapes or records of soothing heartbeat sounds, nature sounds, lullabies, other music

Toys (the possibilities are endless)

Books on baby feeding, baby care, and infant development (see "Recommended Resources")

Choose a Caregiver or Clinic for the Baby

The baby will need a medical caregiver (pediatrician, family physician, nurse practitioner, or health clinic) to provide well-baby care (routine checkups, immunizations) and to treat illnesses if they occur. Get recommendations from friends, the mother's childbirth educator, or her caregiver. You and the mother can interview possible caregivers before the birth, often without charge (when making an appointment for an interview, ask if there will be a fee). The following are important considerations when choosing a caregiver:

- *Location of the office.* How far away is it? There is a real advantage to its being close to home. Traveling a long distance with a sick child can be worrisome.
- *Practical considerations.* What are the caregiver's educational and professional qualifications? What are the fees? Is the practice covered when the caregiver is not available? By whom? At which hospital(s) does the caregiver have privileges?
- *Philosophy of infant health care.* What are the caregiver's attitudes about breastfeeding, introducing solid foods, circumcision, immunizations, feeding and sleeping, day care, and so on?
- *Personal attributes.* Does this caregiver seem kind, competent, and caring? Is this someone you and the mother like and could trust with the baby's health care?

Prepare a Place at Home for the Baby

Whether the baby will have a fully equipped nursery or a corner of a room, you will need to organize space for the baby—for storing clothes, for diaper changing, for sleeping, and for all the equipment that comes along with babies.

Register for Infant-Care or Parenting Classes

Suggest that the mother investigate the available classes and register for any that appeal to her. If you are also the baby's parent, take a class with her. These classes deal with child development, emotional needs of parents and infants, and common problems. Parents learn exercises, songs, and games to play with their children besides having the opportunity to share their concerns with other new parents.

Plan Meals Ahead of Time

Help the mother plan two weeks' worth of meals and do as much food shopping as possible in advance. If a freezer is available, cook food ahead and freeze it for reheating later. You may be surprised to find that simply going to the store or even figuring out what to eat can seem almost overwhelming in the first week after the baby arrives. See chapter 10 for more suggestions about putting together quick, nutritious meals.

Plan to Share Responsibilities

Plan to share the baby-care responsibilities and to take over much of the housework and cooking, or make arrangements for someone else to help. Remember that a baby needs almost constant care for the first few weeks. If the new mother tries to do it all, she will get much less sleep than usual. Full-time newborn care is tiring enough, but because the mother will also be recovering from the physical demands of birth, or possibly from major surgery if she gives birth by cesarean, it may take weeks for her to recover.

Many fathers or partners use vacation time or family leave to stay at home for the first days or weeks to share the work. The baby's grandparents or other relatives can also be a great source of help, as long as the mother's relationship with them is not strained. If the mother and her parents or in-laws do not get along well, their relationship will *not* suddenly improve with the arrival of the baby. Friends can be wonderful about providing meals, running errands, doing chores. Say yes if they offer to help.

On to the Next Step . . .

Once you have prepared as much as possible, enjoy yourselves as you wait for labor to begin. Photograph the expectant mother at the end of her pregnancy; enjoy some evenings out for dinner, movies, concerts, plays, visits with friends and family. Plan enjoyable activities with other children. Make these last days relaxed and enjoyable before your lives change forever.

And now that you know how to really help the expectant mother *before* labor, let's go on to the next step—how you can really help her *during* labor and birth.

Part Two

LABOR AND BIRTH

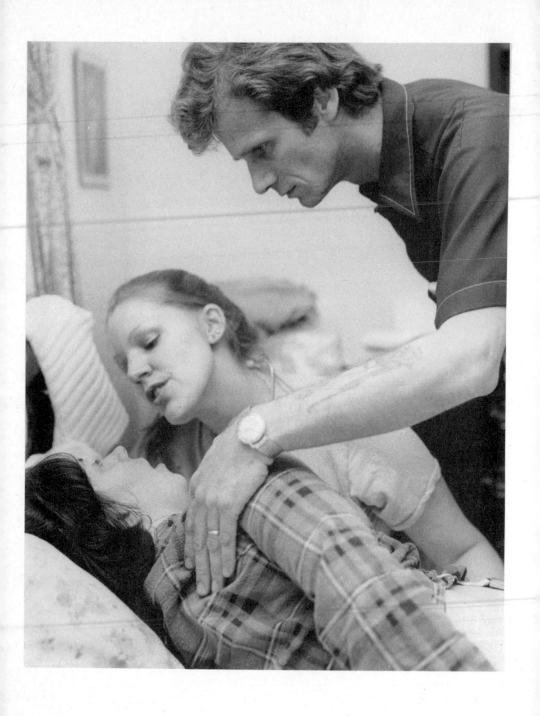

*T*HE PEAK OF PREGNANCY, THE BIRTH OF A BABY, IS AN everyday miracle—part of a day's work for the doctor, midwife, or nurse, but a deep and permanent memory for the birthing woman and those who love her and support her. Your role as the birth partner is to do as much as you can to *help make this birth experience a good memory for her.* She will never forget this birth. She will not only remember many of the events; she will remember and even relive the feelings she had. The kind of care a woman receives and the quality of the support she gets during labor make the difference in whether she looks back on her birth experience with satisfaction and fulfillment or with disappointment and sadness. This is where you come in. Being a birth partner—helping a woman through labor and birth—is clearly a challenge, but it is a challenge that people like you meet all the time.

To be a good birth partner, you need—

- A bond of love or friendship with the mother and a feeling of responsibility toward her.
- Familiarity with her personal preferences and quirks, and with the little things that soothe and relax her.
- Knowledge of what to expect—the physical process of labor, the procedures and interventions commonly used during labor, and when these procedures and interventions are necessary and when they are optional.
- An understanding of the emotional side of labor—the emotional needs of women during labor and the pattern of emotions they usually experience as labor progresses.
- Practical knowledge of how to help in various situations—what to do when.
- Flexibility to adapt to the mother's changing needs during labor. This is "leading by following": how you help, and how much you help, is determined by the mother's needs and responses at the time.

If you also love the mother and the baby, you will care for them in the intimate and personal way that only a husband or loved one can.

The next few chapters will cover the normal birth process and will explain what happens, how the mother responds, what the caregiver does, and how you can help. They will also discuss situations that are particularly difficult for the mother and that are therefore particularly challenging for you. Read these chapters in advance; then use them as an on-the-spot guide during labor.

2

Getting into Labor

*E*veryone wonders how to tell if a woman is in labor. Even for those with vast experience, it is rarely clear exactly when labor starts. Often the mother "sneaks" into labor with unclear, on-again-off-again signs—like an orchestra tuning up before a performance. Then, gradually, she becomes mentally and physically ready for the coordinated effort that eventually results in the birth of the baby. Almost every woman experiences a period of uncertainty and questioning while she awaits clear signs that she is truly in labor.

As long as the two of you eventually put the pieces together, it usually doesn't matter if the mother's labor is vague at the beginning. There is almost always plenty of time, once she is clearly in labor, to get to the hospital or settle in for a home birth. Occasionally, however, a woman is caught by surprise, going into labor earlier or more suddenly than she anticipated. Because of this possibility, you will want to be able to tell the difference between the tuning up (or prelabor) and the real thing (progressing labor).

This chapter will help you both to recognize when the mother is in labor. It explains how she gets into labor both physically and emotionally and describes the role you should play as her birth partner.

The Labor Process

Labor is the process by which a woman gives birth to a baby. The labor process involves the following:

1. Contractions of the uterus, the largest and strongest muscle in the woman's body.
2. Thinning (effacement) and opening (dilation) of the cervix.
3. Breaking of the bag of waters (the membranes or amniotic sac) that surrounds the baby, and the release of the water (amniotic fluid).
4. Descent of the baby out of the uterus and through the birth canal (vagina) to the outside.
5. Birth of the placenta.

Labor usually does not begin until both mother and baby are ready. The last weeks of pregnancy prepare the mother physically and psychologically to give birth, to breastfeed, and to nurture a baby. During this time the baby acquires the "final touches," preparing him or her to handle the stress of labor and to adapt to life outside the uterus.

How Long Will Labor Last?

It is impossible to predict how long any particular labor will last. A perfectly normal labor can take between two and twenty-four hours. In addition, some women experience prelabor contractions for a day or more before labor really begins, that is, before the cervix begins dilating steadily.

Many factors influence the length of labor:

• The strength and frequency of the contractions.
• The condition of the cervix (soft and thin or firm and thick) when contractions begin.
• The size of the baby, particularly the head, in relation to the size of the mother's pelvis.
• The mother's emotional state—if she is lonely, frightened, or angry she may have a longer labor than if she is confident, content, and calm.
• The presentation and position of the baby.

Presentation refers to the part of the baby—top of the head (the vertex), brow, face, buttocks, feet, shoulders—that will be born first. The top of the head almost always *presents* first; problems occur in delivery if any of the others present first.

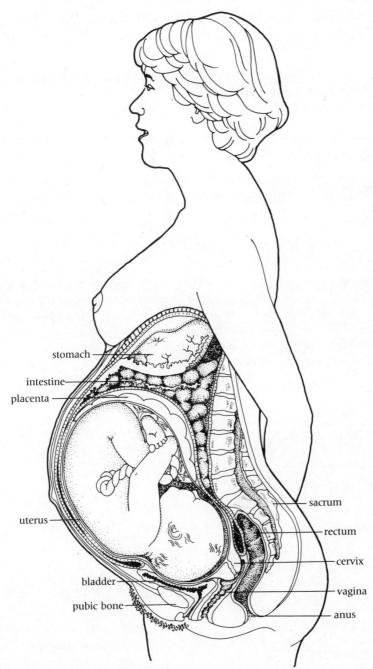

A pregnant woman's anatomy.

Position refers to the placement of the presenting part within the mother's pelvis. The most common positions are *OA* (occiput anterior), *OT* (occiput transverse), and *OP* (occiput posterior):

- OA. The back of the baby's head (the occiput) points toward the mother's front (anterior).
- OT. The back of the baby's head points toward the mother's side (transverse).
- OP. The back of the baby's head points toward the mother's back (posterior).

When the baby is in the OP (occiput posterior) position, labor is sometimes prolonged, and the mother may experience intense backache.

Signs of Labor

How are you going to know when the mother is in labor? A few clues can help you recognize labor long before the birth is imminent. It is equally important, though, to be able to tell when she is *not* in labor. There is nothing more frustrating or disappointing for a woman than thinking she is in labor and discovering, after a trip to the caregiver, that she is not.

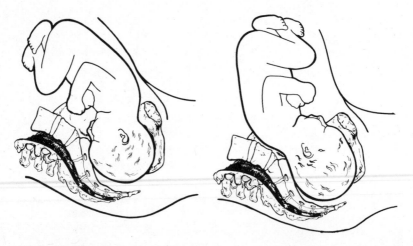

A baby in OP (occiput posterior) position (right) *and OA (occiput anterior) position (* left).

If you both know the signs of labor (see the table on pages 38–39) and how to interpret them, you will be more likely to react appropriately. Some of these signs are more definite than others. They are categorized as Possible Signs, Preliminary Signs, and Positive Signs.

- *Possible Signs.* Without other signs, these are not clear enough to get excited about. They may be due to something besides labor, such as indigestion, fatigue, or physical overexertion. They reassure you that the mother is moving in the right direction, but that is usually their only significance. If, however, the mother has had a rapid labor with a previous birth, she should be particularly alert to the Possible Signs to avoid being surprised by another rapid labor.
- *Preliminary Signs.* These are more important than the Possible Signs, but it could still be hours or even days before labor is really underway.
- *Positive Signs.* These are the only certain signs that the mother is in progressing or "true" labor.

If you are aware of these signs of labor, chances are very good that you will be able to correctly interpret what is going on. Sometimes, though, couples need the help of the caregiver to figure out if the mother is really in labor or not.

CAUTION: If the mother experiences noticeable contractions (every fifteen minutes or less) for more than two hours, combined with *any* of the other labor signs *more than three weeks before her due date,* she should tell her caregiver. She might be in *premature labor,* which can sometimes be stopped if it is caught early. If she is beyond thirty-seven weeks of pregnancy, she should wait for the Positive Signs before calling her caregiver.

If the Bag of Waters Breaks before Labor Begins

If the mother's bag of waters breaks (if water is leaking or flowing from her vagina) before labor begins, make the following observations to report to her caregiver:

1. The *amount* of fluid. Is it a trickle or a gush?
2. The *color* of the fluid. Normally, the fluid is clear. If it is pink

SIGNS OF LABOR

Signs and Symptoms	Comments
Possible Signs	
Vague nagging backache causing restlessness—a need to keep changing positions.	• Different from backache commonly experienced during pregnancy. • May be associated with early contractions.
Several soft bowel movements—sometimes accompanied by flulike, "sick" feelings.	• Probably associated with increase in hormonelike substances in the bloodsteam (prostaglandins). These substances soften and thin the cervix.
Intermittent or continuous cramps, similar to menstrual cramps; discomfort may extend to thighs.	• May be associated with prostaglandin action and early contractions.
Unusual burst of energy resulting in great activity; termed the "nesting urge."	• Ensures that the mother will have strength and energy to handle labor (but she should try to curb exhausting activity).
Preliminary Signs	
Blood-tinged mucous discharge ("show" or mucous plug) released from the vagina; mother continues passing this discharge off and on throughout labor.	• Associated with thinning of the cervix. • May occur days before other signs or not until after progressing contractions have begun. • A discharge, often mistaken for show, may also appear within a day after a prenatal pelvic examination and is not a sign of labor. Show is pink or red; the discharge after a pelvic exam tends to be brownish.

or red, there might be bleeding into the fluid. If it is brownish or greenish, the baby may have emptied his bowels (passed meconium), which happens when a baby is stressed in the uterus. Such stress is caused by a temporary lack of oxygen.

3. The *odor* of the fluid. Normally, the fluid is practically odorless. If it has a foul smell, there may be an infection within the uterus, which could spread to the baby.

This information helps the caregiver plan what to do next—have the mother stay home, come in for an examination, or go to the hospital.

SIGNS OF LABOR—*Continued*

Signs and Symptoms	Comments
Bag of waters leaks, resulting in a trickle of fluid from the vagina, but no contractions occur. (See "If the Bag of Waters Breaks before Labor Begins," page 37.)	• Not necessarily associated with spontaneous labor, although softening of the cervix may hasten after the bag of waters begins leaking. • Occurs before labor only about 10 to 12 percent of the time.
Continuing, nonprogressing contractions that do *not* become longer, stronger, and closer together over a period of time. Sometimes called "false" labor, prelabor, or Braxton-Hicks contractions. (See "The Concept of 'False' Labor," page 40.)	• Accomplishes softening and thinning of cervix, allowing cervix to begin dilating. • Should not be perceived as unproductive.

Positive Signs

Progressing contractions, which are contractions that become longer, stronger, and closer together over time.	• It is a clear sign that the cervix is opening if the mother has had ten to twelve contractions that (1) average one minute in length, (2) occur five or fewer minutes apart, and (3) feel painful or "very strong." • It is an even clearer sign if these contractions are combined with show (blood-tinged discharge). • The mother cannot be distracted from these contractions. • She may feel these contractions in her abdomen or back, or both.
Spontaneous breaking of bag of waters (rupture of membranes) with pop or gush of fluid followed by progressing contractions within hours. (See "If the Bag of Waters Breaks before Labor Begins," page 37.)	• Often associated with rapid labor. • Usually happens in late labor. Rupture of membranes occurs before other signs of labor only about 10 percent of the time.

Also, once the bag of waters has broken, the mother should take the following precautions to prevent bacteria from entering her uterus, increasing the chance of infection:

1. She should put nothing in her vagina: she should not use tampons; she should not have intercourse; she should not check her cervix with her fingers; and she should not take a tub bath, since bath water could enter her vagina. (The last precaution is not accepted by all caregivers. Some believe a bath in her own tub is not risky.)

2. Take the mother's temperature every few hours. If it rises above normal, the caregiver needs to know, as this may signal infection.

3. The caregiver and nurses should be very cautious about doing vaginal exams. Exams tend to push bacteria up into the uterus and increase the chances of infection. Vaginal exams are often done out of curiosity—simply to find out if the cervix has changed. With a broken bag of waters, it is safer to restrict vaginal exams to situations in which (a) a decision needs to be made about how to proceed (for example, whether to induce labor—start labor with medications— or allow the mother to walk, and so forth), *and* (b) the decision depends on how much the cervix has already changed or on other factors that can be determined only with a vaginal exam.

If you and the mother follow these precautions and make the appropriate observations, the mother can probably safely wait for labor to begin spontaneously, and the caregiver probably won't think that it is necessary to induce labor. This, however, is a management decision that you and the mother need to discuss with the caregiver, preferably in advance, when you go over the Birth Plan. Most caregivers have a policy regarding their management of ruptured membranes (broken bag of waters); some want to induce labor within hours after the bag breaks, whereas others wait. It is wise to find out this policy ahead of time and try to change it if the mother is uncomfortable with it.

CAUTION: On very rare occasions, the baby's cord slips out of the uterus as the water escapes. This is called *prolapsed cord* and is a *true emergency*. See "Prolapsed Cord," page 153.

The Concept of "False" Labor

Frequently, women have contractions that seem quite strong and frequent, but when examined they are told they are in *"false" labor*, which means *the cervix is not yet opening (dilating)*. These contractions, called Braxton-Hicks contractions, may occur frequently in late pregnancy. Besides being discouraged, many women in "false" labor feel embarrassed or worried, and they may lose faith in their ability to recognize labor. The kind of labor support the mother receives under these circumstances is critical to her ability to cope with "true" progressing labor later on. Here is how you can help:

- It is most important to point out that "false" labor does *not* mean that what the mother is experiencing is not real. All it means is that her cervix has not yet begun to open.
- Remind her that opening (dilation) of the cervix beyond about two centimeters is one of the *last* things to happen in labor. The fact that her cervix is not yet opening does *not* mean that she is not making progress.
- If the mother becomes discouraged with a prolonged period of little or no apparent progress, remind her of the six ways (see list below) her body may be progressing.
- Ask the caregiver who examines the mother if the cervix has moved forward, if it has softened further, or if it has thinned more (see "Labor Progresses in Six Ways"). Sometimes the caregiver is so focused on the opening of the cervix (dilation), he or she fails to mention these other important signs of progress.
- See "Prelabor," page 48, and "The Slow-to-Start Labor," page 97, for some strategies to help her cope with "false" labor.

You can be sure that if the mother has either of the Positive Signs of labor listed in the table on page 39, her cervix is opening. She cannot be in "false" labor if, over a period of time, her contractions have become longer *and* stronger *and* closer together. See "Timing Contractions," page 44.

Labor Progresses in Six Ways

A woman makes progress toward birth in the following ways, even though she is not said to be in "true," progressing labor until her body reaches step 4.

1. *The cervix softens (ripens).* While still thick, the cervix, through the action of hormones and substances called prostaglandins, softens and becomes more pliable.

2. *The position of the cervix changes.* The cervix points toward the mother's back during most of pregnancy, then gradually moves forward. The position of the cervix is assessed by a vaginal exam and is described as posterior (pointing toward the back) or anterior (pointing toward) the front.

3. *The cervix thins (effaces).* The cervix, usually about one and a half inches thick, gradually becomes paper-thin. The amount of thinning (effacement) is measured in percentages: 0 percent means no thinning

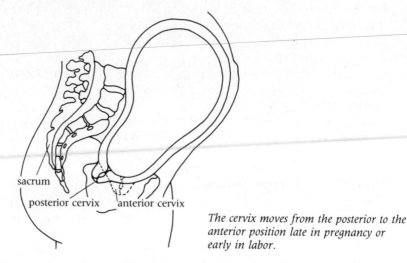

sacrum

posterior cervix   anterior cervix

The cervix moves from the posterior to the anterior position late in pregnancy or early in labor.

has occurred; 50 percent means the cervix is about half its former thickness; 100 percent means it is paper-thin.

4. *The cervix opens (dilates).* The opening (dilation) of the cervix usually occurs with contractions when the woman is in established labor—after the cervix has undergone the changes described above. Dilation is measured in centimeters (one centimeter equals almost one-half inch), and it is common for the cervix to be dilated one to three centimeters before the woman has any signs of labor. The cervix must open approximately ten centimeters in diameter to allow the baby through.

5. *The baby's head rotates.* This rotation makes it easier for the baby to pass through the birth canal. (Sometimes the head must "mold" before it can rotate. This means that the head changes shape, becoming longer and thinner. Molding is normal, although some babies' heads look somewhat misshapen for a day or two following birth, after which time the head returns to a round shape.) The most favorable position for birth is usually the OA (occiput anterior) position.

6. *The baby descends.* The baby descends through the cervix, the pelvis, and the vagina to the outside. The descent is described in terms of "station," which (a) tells how far above or below the mother's mid-pelvis is the baby's head (or buttocks, in the case of a breech presentation—see page 113 for more information about breech presentation); (b) is measured in centimeters; and (c) ranges from "mi-

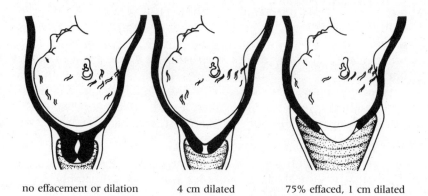

no effacement or dilation   4 cm dilated   75% effaced, 1 cm dilated

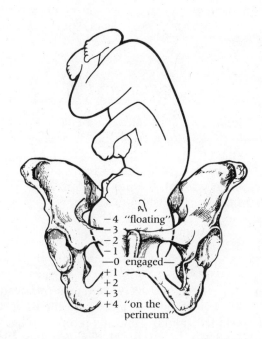

−4 "floating"
−3
−2
−1
—0 engaged—
+1
+2
+3
+4 "on the perineum"

Station—a measure of the baby's descent.

nus 4" to "plus 4" ("0 station" means the baby's head is right at the mother's mid-pelvis). "Minus 1, 2, 3, or 4" means the head is that number of centimeters above the mid-pelvis. The greater the "plus" number, the closer the baby's head is to the outside and to being born.

Some descent takes place before labor begins, especially with first-time mothers. When the baby *drops*, it settles into the pelvis. Most descent, however, does not occur until late in labor.

Steps 4 to 6 (dilation, rotation, and descent) really cannot take place until the first three steps are well underway. In other words, a cervix that is firm, thick, or posterior won't open. It simply is not ready. And, a baby won't rotate and descend significantly until the cervix is open. For many women the first three steps take place imperceptibly and gradually in late pregnancy. For others they take place all at once, with hours or days of frequent and sometimes strong contractions, referred to as "false" labor, "prelabor," or Braxton-Hicks contractions.

Timing Contractions

One of the important jobs of the birth partner is to time contractions. Since changes in the length, strength, and frequency of contractions are the all-important hallmarks of true, progressing labor, it is a good idea for you to (1) know how to time correctly and (2) keep a written record. Then, when you call the mother's caregiver, you will have accurate and concrete information to provide.

Time contractions in this way:

1. Use a watch or clock with a second hand.
2. Use a written form similar to the sample "Early Labor Record," page 45.
3. You do not need to time every contraction. Instead, time and record four or five contractions in a row and then stop for a while (a few minutes to a few hours). Time and record another four or five contractions later when the mother thinks they have changed or if she has had some of the other signs of labor.
4. Always note the time each contraction begins (specify A.M. or P.M.). Record this time in the column headed "Time Contraction Starts."
5. Time the length of each contraction (in seconds), and record this time in the column headed "Duration." Knowing when a con-

EARLY LABOR RECORD

Date _____

Time Contraction Starts	Duration (seconds)	Frequency (minutes from start of one to start of next)	Comments (strength, foods eaten, breathing pattern, discharge, etc.)

traction begins and ends is tricky. There are two ways: (a) the mother signals when she feels the contraction begin and end, or (b) you place your fingertips high on her uterus and begin timing when you feel the uterus become harder and rise slightly (it feels like your biceps muscle when you contract it); time the contraction until you cannot feel the hardness anymore.

Sometimes the birth partner cannot feel the contractions well or can only barely feel them. The mother can usually feel them for longer, from the "inside," than can the birth partner or even a nurse, who from the "outside" probably feels only the peak. Compare the mother's assessments with yours; tell her caregiver if they differ significantly (for example, you might say "She feels them lasting for ninety seconds, but I can feel them for only thirty."). When there is a large discrepancy, the other information on the "Early Labor Record" and the caregiver's knowledge of the mother's condition become more important in determining how labor is progressing.

6. Figure out how frequently the contractions are coming by subtracting the time at the start of one contraction from the time at the start of the next. Record the number of minutes between contractions in the "Frequency" column. (For example, if one contraction begins at 7:32 and the next one begins at 7:45, they are thirteen minutes apart.) Do the same for each subsequent contraction.

7. In the "Comments" column, record any other significant events: how strong the contractions seem now compared with earlier; the mother's appetite and what she has eaten; if she is using patterned breathing (see page 85); if she has back pain or blood-tinged discharge; if fluid is leaking or gushing; how she is coping.

8. When you call her caregiver, be prepared to report the items on the "Early Labor Record." Have it near the phone.

9. See page 52 for the discussion, "When Do You Go to the Hospital or Settle In at Home?"

TIMING CONTRACTIONS

3

Moving through the Stages of Labor

The medical profession has established the following terms to describe what is happening during labor and how the mother is progressing:

- *Prelabor* describes the time before actual labor begins, when the mother is having contractions but the cervix isn't dilating. Prelabor is sometimes referred to as "false labor."
- The *first stage* of labor is the *dilation stage*, during which the cervix dilates completely—to about ten centimeters in diameter.
- The *second stage* is the *birthing stage*, during which the baby is born.
- The *third stage* is the *placental stage*, during which the placenta, or afterbirth, is born.

The dilation (first) and birthing (second) stages are further subdivided into three phases each. With every new phase, labor changes its rhythm, and the mother must make an emotional adjustment. This chapter describes each stage and phase, and includes suggestions about how you can help the mother cope. See the table "Normal Labor—in a Nutshell," pages 70–72, for a brief summary of this information.

Prelabor

What Is It? During prelabor ("false" labor), the mother has off-and-on uterine contractions and the uterus begins "tuning up." The cervix softens, moves forward, and thins. Contractions may be regular and strong, sometimes even painful, for hours. However, they do not progress (by becoming longer, stronger, and closer together) and they may stop. The cervix is not yet dilating—the sign that she is truly in labor.

Prelabor is sometimes confusing to the mother, to her birth partner, and even to her caregiver. You may find if difficult to distinguish between this tuning up and the "real thing." Then, without warning, and often without the mother recognizing it, prelabor becomes the "real thing": the contractions become longer, stronger, and closer together, and the cervix begins to dilate.

How Long Does It Last? Prelabor may come and go over several hours, days, or even weeks.

How Will the Mother Feel? During prelabor, the mother may feel one or more of these emotions:

- *Confusion,* about whether she is in labor or not.
- *Excitement and anticipation,* as she tells everyone she's in labor.
- *Fear,* especially if she is not mentally prepared, if labor is earlier than she expected, or if her contractions are more painful than she expected.

If prelabor goes on for days or weeks (the slow-to-start labor), the mother may feel one or more of these emotions:

- *Frustration,* over not knowing what is happening and feeling tricked by the confusing signs.
- *Discouragement,* over the long wait.
- *Fatigue,* if she has missed sleep.
- *Doubt or anxiety,* about her body's ability to function properly, especially if the contractions are painful but not progressing (getting longer, stronger, and closer together).
- *Worry,* about being too tired to handle "true" (progressing) labor when it begins.

What Does the Caregiver Do? The caregiver may suggest that the mother wait at home, come in for a check of progress, or go straight to the hospital. In addition, the caregiver may do any of the following:

- Come to the home to check the mother if the birth is to take place there.
- Offer advice and encouragement to help her handle this frustrating phase.
- Offer drugs or alcohol for rest or to slow contractions (see "Medications for Pain during Labor," page 161).
- Try to speed labor with drugs or by breaking the bag of waters (see "Induction or Augmentation of Labor," page 135).

How Can You Help? Help the mother with prelabor in these ways:

- Realize that a long prelabor is not a medical problem in itself. Therefore, it is mostly up to the two of you to handle it.
- Recognize prelabor for what it is. Help the mother determine whether her contractions are progressing by *timing* them. (See "Timing Contractions," page 44; "Signs of Labor," page 36; and "The Concept of 'False' Labor," page 40.)
- Check with the caregiver for advice and reassurance, and possibly to arrange for an examination.
- Consult "The Slow-to-Start Labor," page 97, for specific coping techniques if prelabor continues for a long time

Dilation

What Is It? Dilation is the first stage of labor. In fact, medical people refer to it as the *first stage.* It begins when the prelabor contractions change their pattern and start getting longer, stronger, and closer together. It ends when the cervix has dilated completely (to approximately ten centimeters). It can proceed very quickly or rather slowly. The dilation stage has distinct phases: the latent phase (early labor); the active phase (active labor); and the transition phase (transition).

The line between prelabor and the dilation stage is rarely clear, so don't expect that you or the mother will know the moment her cervix begins to open.

In a typical labor, the contractions gradually and steadily increase in intensity and duration and come closer together. Early contractions may last thirty or forty seconds and come every fifteen to twenty minutes. Although there are exceptions, these early contractions are *usually not* painful. But by the time the cervix has opened to eight or nine centimeters, the contractions may last ninety seconds, feel very intense (almost surely very painful), and come every two to four minutes.

Occasionally, labor does not follow this predictable pattern. Sometimes the early contractions are very painful and progress very quickly. If that is the case, there will be no time for you to use the following information. Skip to "The Very Rapid Labor," page 99, for help with this special situation.

How Long Does It Last? The dilation stage lasts from two to twenty-four hours. However, for first-time mothers it is rare for the dilation stage to last less than six to eight hours.

You cannot know in advance how long dilation will take. Therefore, prepare yourselves for the whole range of possibilities: be able to handle the short, intense labor or to pace yourselves through the extra-long one. (See "The Very Rapid Labor," page 99; "The Slow-to-Start Labor," page 97; and "Failure to Progress," page 150.)

When Should You Call the Caregiver? Call the mother's caregiver under any of the following circumstances:

- If the mother has possible premature labor (see "Signs of Labor," page 36).
- If she has leaking or a gush of fluid (see "If the Bag of Waters Breaks before Labor Begins," page 37).
- When the mother's contractions are clearly becoming longer, stronger, and closer together (see "Signs of Labor," page 36, and "Timing Contractions," page 44).
- Whenever you or the mother has questions or concerns.
- If the mother has had a child before, she should call the caregiver or hospital whenever she thinks or knows she's in labor. A second (or later) labor is usually faster than the mother's first one.

Early Labor

What Is It? The early labor phase (or early labor) is a subdivision of the dilation stage, and it begins when dilation begins. It lasts until the cervix is dilated to four or five centimeters. Medical professionals call this the *latent phase* of the first stage.

The big difference between prelabor and early labor is that during early labor the cervix begins to gradually open. Progressing contractions are the mother's best sign that early labor has begun. The caregiver uses vaginal exams to determine changes in the cervix during this phase.

How Long Does It Last? Early labor usually takes from two-thirds to three-quarters of the total time of the dilation stage. In other words, it could take from a few hours to twenty hours or so for a woman to reach four centimeters of dilation. The length of early labor depends largely on the state of the cervix and on the position and station of the baby within the pelvis at the time labor begins. Chances for normal progress are increased if the following conditions exist:

- The cervix is very soft and thin.
- The baby is in the occiput anterior (OA) position, with its head down, its chin on its chest, and the back of its head toward the mother's front (see page 36).
- The baby is low in the mother's pelvis (see page 42).

Under these conditions, the mother probably will have an average or shorter-than-average early labor. Under any other conditions, early labor is likely to take longer.

How Will the Mother Feel? The mother's response to early labor is not all that different from her response to prelabor. She is still uncertain. She still wants and looks for the positive signs of labor.

Getting into labor emotionally takes time. How the mother adjusts will depend on the circumstances—whether labor is early, on time, or late, for example, and whether early contractions are hard and fast or vague and slow.

Reactions to labor vary from relief, elation, or excitement to denial, disbelief, or panic. As labor settles into a rhythmic pattern, the mother settles down emotionally, pacing herself and finding routines for handling each contraction.

Sometimes, in the excitement of early labor, the mother *rushes the labor along in her mind*. She may overreact or become preoccupied with every contraction. This results partly from her desire for labor to go quickly and partly from the unclear signs of early labor. She may become convinced that her labor is progressing more rapidly than it really is.

What sometimes happens if she rushes the labor mentally is that you go to the hospital too early, she starts using patterned breathing and other labor-coping measures before they are really needed, and you both start speculating that her cervix is dilated much more than it really is. Then she becomes discouraged when she has a vaginal exam and finds that she's not nearly as advanced in labor as she thought she was.

How can you tell if the mother is (1) overreacting to early labor or (2) having a particularly difficult or rapid labor? Without vaginal exams, you cannot really know whether labor is progressing quickly or not. The best you can do is make an educated guess. Refer to "Signs of Labor" (page 36), time the contractions, and see if the mother can be distracted. Try a walk outside, or phoning or visiting with friends or relatives. If labor seems to "slow down" or become easier when the mother is distracted, she may have overreacted. Keep up the distractions. (See "How You Can Help," page 53, for other ideas for handling an overreaction to early labor.) If, however, labor does not "slow down" when you try to distract her, the mother is not overreacting. Stop trying to distract her and, instead, work with her on handling this intense labor. (See "The Very Rapid Labor," page 99, for suggestions.)

What Does the Caregiver Do? During early labor, the caregiver can help in the following ways:

- By giving advice over the telephone. When you call, be prepared to provide the information recorded on the Early-Labor Record (page 45).
- By helping the mother decide when to go to the hospital or, if she is having a home birth, when to settle in at home for the labor.
- By doing a vaginal exam to give you both an idea of how the labor is progressing.

When Do You Go to the Hospital or Settle In at Home? Under most circumstances, the first-time mother should go to the hospital or, if the birth will be at home, settle in there when she has had *ten to twelve* consecutive contractions that—

- Last at least one minute or more.
- Average five or fewer minutes apart.
- Are strong enough that she *must* use patterned breathing (page 85).
- Are strong enough that she cannot be distracted from them.

It will take you and the mother about an hour to time these contractions and determine whether they fit this pattern.

Sometimes there are special reasons for the mother to go to the hospital earlier. For example:

- The mother lives a long distance from the hospital.
- The mother has medical problems that require early admission. Her caregiver should advise her if these problems exist.

- The mother has had a child before and thinks or knows she is in labor. A woman's second (or later) labor usually goes faster than her first one did.
- She simply feels more secure in the hospital.

Because early labor can take so long, it is often a good idea to spend the time relaxing together by yourselves or with friends until the mother's contractions fit the pattern described here. It is usually best not to arrive at the hospital (or call the caregiver to the home) too early because—

- The mother may feel "performance anxiety"—pressure to start producing some good contractions. With the caregiver or nurse hovering and waiting for something to happen, she may feel embarrassed that labor is so slow.
- The mother may become preoccupied with the contractions and the apparent lack of progress, making labor seem longer or more difficult than it is.
- The mother may become bored or anxious; she may become predisposed to using inappropriate medical interventions to speed up this normally slow part of labor.

Sometimes the caregiver will suggest that the mother leave the hospital and come back later. For a home birth, everyone except you may have to leave for a while. Although discouraging, these measures allow the labor to settle into its own pattern and take pressure off the mother.

How Can You Help? Your role now is not very different from the role you played during prelabor; you can help in these ways:

- Remain close by.
- Time the contractions, as described on pages 44–46.
- Help the mother pass the time with pleasant and distracting activities. Refer to the activities suggested for "The Slow-to-Start Labor," page 97.
- Discuss with the mother whether you should leave for work, errands, or other activities. Your decision should be based on her feelings and the following considerations:

    Are you always accessible by phone? Some birth partners rent a beeper (see "Paging Systems" in the Yellow Pages) for a few weeks before the due date so they will always be within reach.

    How far do you have to travel to reach the mother? How long will it take you?

Is there someone else available (a friend, a relative, a neighbor) to help out if the mother needs someone right away?

What are the pressures on you—from work, school, or other responsibilities? Will a few more hours let you clear up pressing obligations?

If you feel you should leave, and the mother agrees, be sure someone else sits in for you until you are free. This should be a last resort.

When the mother becomes preoccupied with the contractions— she cannot walk or talk through them without pausing—it is no longer appropriate to distract her. Instead, you now need to do the following:

- Continue to time the contractions (see pages 44–46).
- Give the mother your undivided attention throughout every contraction. Stop what you are doing and stop talking so you can focus on her. Do not ask her questions during contractions.
- Watch her during the contractions and help her to relax her entire body during each one (see "Relaxation," page 83).
- Suggest that she begin using patterned breathing (see page 85).
- Help her decide when to call her caregiver.

Early labor eventually settles into a clear pattern of contractions, resulting in the more rapid dilation of the cervix—the active labor phase.

Active Labor

What Is It? The active phase of labor (or active labor) begins when the cervix has dilated to four or five centimeters and lasts until it reaches about eight centimeters. During active labor the rhythm and pace of labor change, and the mother's cervix opens more steadily and more rapidly than it did during early labor. The cervix is now so thin and soft that it offers much less resistance to dilation.

Contractions tend to be clear cut, consistently lasting at least a full minute and averaging four to five minutes apart. They are usually very intense, and most women describe them as painful.

How Long Does It Last? Normally, active labor is shorter than early labor. For first-time mothers, active labor usually ranges from two to six hours. It is usually much faster for mothers who have had babies before—from twenty minutes to three hours.

What Does the Mother Feel? The mother must make an emotional adjustment to the changing rhythm of labor for the following reasons:

- Labor has already continued for a relatively long time; prelabor and early labor may have been going on for hours or even for days.
- Then, when she is feeling that labor is very long, it also becomes more painful as the contractions pick up in strength and frequency.
- The mother does not yet realize why the contractions are increasing. She is not aware that her labor is probably speeding up. She will not know that until some time has passed and she has made more progress.

The mother may respond to the changing rhythm of labor in the following ways:

- She may feel tired and discouraged as she realizes that the tough part is just beginning. She may lose confidence in her ability to cope with these more frequent, intense contractions.
- Her sense of humor fades. Your funniest jokes don't amuse her.
- Extraneous conversation becomes annoying. She may feel very alone if you and others do not recognize this change and continue trying to distract her, or, worse yet, ignore her.
- She becomes serious and focused on herself and her contractions. It is about all she can handle to relax and breathe during her contractions. When a contraction ends, most of her conversation is centered on reviewing it with you and talking about what to do for the next one.
- She becomes quiet; the room becomes quiet.
- For many women, the active labor phase is their "moment of truth": suddenly it sinks in that this labor is real; there is no way out except to keep going and have the baby. Realizing this may frighten or depress her at first, but with help from you she can accept and yield to the labor, and work with it instead of trying to control it.

What Does the Caregiver Do? Unless there is a problem, the doctor is seldom at the bedside during active labor, but is available nearby or by telephone. A nurse provides most of the bedside care, following the doctor's orders. If the caregiver is a midwife, she usually provides care herself; otherwise, a nurse carries out the midwife's orders.

During active labor, the midwife or nurse remains close by and becomes more actively involved. Now that progress is faster and the contractions are more intense, closer surveillance is needed. The nurse or the midwife frequently checks—

- The mother's blood pressure, pulse, and temperature
- Her fluid intake and urine output
- The amount of dilation of her cervix
- The fetal heart rate
- The quality, intensity, and frequency of the contractions
- Other signs

Routines vary depending on the management style of the caregiver. Some caregivers rely heavily on interventions and medical technology. For example, they might break the bag of waters, keep the mother in bed, give intravenous (IV) fluids, use electronic monitors to check the fetus and the contractions, and give the mother medications to relieve pain. Other caregivers rely on simpler methods. They might encourage the mother to drink liquids and move around, listen to the fetal heartbeat with a stethoscope or a hand-held ultrasound device, and suggest comfort measures (page 73) to relieve pain. See the introduction to part 3, and chapter 6, for information about commonly used tests and procedures, as well as for questions to ask and alternatives to consider.

The nurse or the caregiver also offers advice and reassurance. Having someone there with expertise and experience—someone you both trust—can be immensely reassuring. Don't hesitate to ask for help or advice if you feel uncertain about the labor or about how you can help the mother.

How Can You Help? Your role during active labor is very important. How you respond to the mother's needs determines to a large extent how well she copes and how satisfied with her labor experience she will feel later. Here are some guidelines for helping the mother during this phase.

- *Be sure the staff is aware of her Birth Plan.*
- *Follow the mother's lead.* Take your cues from her; match her mood. When she becomes serious or quiet, you should become serious or quiet. Don't try to cheer her up or jolly her out of this mood.

  Do not continue trying to distract her. The labor takes almost all her attention, and she needs you with her both physically and emotionally.
- *Give the mother your undivided attention* throughout every contraction, even if her eyes are closed and she seems not to need it. Do not chat with others in the room, and discourage others from engaging in nonessential conversation. Such talk could make the mother feel very alone and ignored, even if she is coping well. Help her to

remain relaxed and use patterned breathing through each contraction (see "Relaxation," page 83, and "Patterned Breathing," page 85).

- *Develop "rituals."* A *ritual*, in labor, is a series of comforting actions, repeated during every contraction. Some rituals are planned in advance; others are discovered on the spot during labor. The basic ritual for handling contractions includes relaxation, attention focusing, and patterned breathing, as well as any of the many comfort measures described on pages 73–92 that appeal to the mother. Try to include as part of the ritual reminders to sip fluid after each contraction and empty her bladder every hour or two.

Don't be surprised when other unexpected and unplanned personal touches (for example, speaking in a certain tone of voice, repeating particular words or phrases, touching the mother in a certain way in a certain spot, close eye contact, a series of movements) become vital parts of the labor ritual. That is what usually happens. (See "Rituals," page 74, for examples of rituals that others have created.)

Stick with the same ritual for as long as it helps. Don't be afraid to try something new if the mother is not responding well. She will let you know if she wants to go back to the previous ritual.

Transition

What Is It? The transition phase is a turning point in labor; it is the period of transition from the dilation to the birthing stage. Professionals call this the transition from the first to the second stage because the mother's body seems to be partly in the dilation (first) stage and partly in the birthing (second) stage.

During the transition phase the cervix dilates the last two centimeters or so (from about eight centimeters to about ten) to complete the dilation (first) stage of labor. At this time, the baby begins to descend—the head moves from the uterus through the cervix and down into the vagina—to begin the birthing (second) stage of labor. Contractions usually feel very intense, last one and a half to two minutes, and occur very close together.

Sometimes a "lip" of cervix remains. A "lip" occurs when a part of the cervix remains thickened even after the cervix is almost completely dilated. The presence of a lip seems to delay the last bit of dilation. It takes several contractions before the cervix eases back to let the baby's head through.

The uterus may begin its expulsive efforts even before the cervix is completely dilated. We call this the "urge to push." It makes the mother catch her breath, grunt, or hold her breath and strain; this is what is meant by the terms "pushing" and "bearing down." The urge to push is involuntary; she does not make it happen and cannot prevent it from happening. Yet if the cervix is not completely dilated, it may be better if she tries to avoid bearing down with her urge. The mother can avoid bearing down by raising her chin and blowing rapidly and lightly. She may be asked to do this by the nurse or caregiver. Pushing too hard too soon may cause the cervix to swell and cause the labor to slow. (See "Avoiding Pushing," page 89.)

How Long Does It Last? The transition usually takes from five to twenty-five contractions; it lasts from fifteen minutes to an hour and fifteen minutes. If a lip of cervix remains, the transition phase is likely to take longer.

What Does the Mother Feel? Transition is often the most difficult part of labor for the mother. The combined physical sensations of intense, frequent contractions and of the baby's head moving down may cause her legs, or even her whole body, to tremble. She may feel nauseated and may vomit. She may feel cramps in her thighs or pressure in her pelvis. She may feel she is passing a bowel movement. She may feel very hot, then cold. She may weep or cry out, feeling that she cannot handle any more, that it will never end. She may feel overwhelmed, and react angrily, saying, "Don't touch me! My skin hurts!" or "I can't go on!" or "Stop doing that!" Or, instead, she may withdraw into herself, dozing between contractions and moaning, groaning, or whimpering during them, all the while relaxing her body quite well.

What Does the Caregiver Do? During the transition phase, a nurse or a midwife is in constant attendance. The doctor is not necessarily with the mother, although when informed that the mother is approaching delivery, the doctor soon comes.

The nurse or the midwife does the following:

- Checks the cervix if she needs to confirm the mother's progress in labor
- Asks the mother not to push or to push only gently if the cervix is not fully opened
- Offers reassurance that the mother is all right and that labor is moving rapidly

- Helps you in your role as birth partner and reassures *you* that the mother is all right and behaving normally
- Begins preparations for the birth

If the birth will take place in the same room where the mother is laboring, the nurse or the midwife brings in the equipment necessary for the delivery and for the immediate care of the baby. If the birth is to take place in the delivery room, the staff prepares to take the mother there, bed and all. Be sure to go along!

This is an exciting moment, when everyone begins preparing for the infant. Finally, even the staff is acting as if a baby is really coming!

How Can You Help? Your role during transition is all important. You can truly take some of the mother's burden if you know what to do:

- Stay calm. Your touch should be firm and confident. Your voice should remain calm and encouraging.
- Stay close to the mother with your face near hers.
- If she is panicky and scared, go into your "Take-Charge Routine" (page 94).
- Remind her that this difficult phase is short, and that she is almost in the birthing stage.
- Remind yourself that it is *normal* for the transition phase to be difficult, that the mother's mood will improve when her cervix is fully dilated, and that if you are to reassure her you must not worry about her. Her behavior is not abnormal; her pain is not more than one should expect at this time. The rest of labor will not be this intense.
- What about pain medications? If the mother has planned to use pain medications during labor, she can take them now (use the "Pain Medications Preference Scale," pages 164–165, to guide your decisions). If she has wanted to avoid pain medications, then do not mention them. Instead, help her get through this phase without them, as tough as it may be.
- Be sure the nurse or caregiver knows if the mother has an urge to push (page 58). The caregiver will check the mother's progress to determine if pushing is appropriate.
- Help the mother to avoid pushing, if the caregiver says she isn't ready yet, or to push when she feels the urge, if her cervix is fully opened. (See "Breathing Patterns for Pushing," page 89, for advice on helping her push or avoid pushing, as appropriate.)

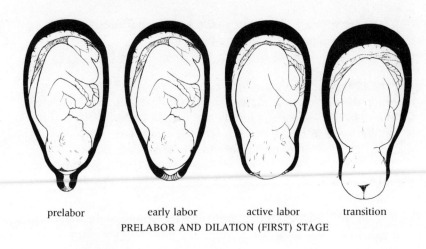

prelabor   early labor   active labor   transition

PRELABOR AND DILATION (FIRST) STAGE

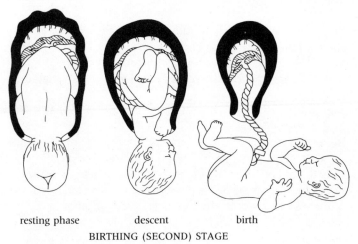

resting phase   descent   birth

BIRTHING (SECOND) STAGE

The baby rotates and descends as the cervix opens.

Descent and Birth

What Is It? The birthing stage, or stage of descent, begins when the cervix is fully dilated and ends with the birth of the baby. Medical professionals call it the *second stage*.

During the birthing stage the mother works very hard: she bears down—actively pushes—by holding her breath and straining with the urge to push that comes several times in every contraction. In this way she works with her uterus to press the baby down and out.

The birthing stage has three distinct phases: the resting, the descent, and the crowning and birth (see the illustration). Each phase is characterized by different physical developments, and each requires that the mother make an emotional adjustment.

The management of the birthing (second) stage varies among caregivers. Some want to speed the baby's descent along as fast as possible, whereas others feel it is better to let the labor go at its own pace as long as mother and baby appear to be doing well.

How Long Does It Last? A normal birthing stage may last from fifteen minutes (three to five contractions) to three hours or more. For most first-time mothers, the birthing stage is completed in less than two hours; for women who have given birth before, in less than one hour.

The Resting Phase

What Is It? The resting phase is an apparent pause in the labor. Although not all women experience it, you and the mother should both be ready for it.

The resting phase is a "catch-up break" for the uterus; it comes after the cervix is completely dilated and the baby's head has passed through the cervix into the birth canal. The uterus had been tightly stretched around the baby before the head slipped out. Now, suddenly, only the baby's body remains inside the uterus and the uterus fits more loosely around the baby. The uterus needs time to catch up, to tighten around the rest of the baby.

This tightening occurs imperceptibly. The muscle fibers in the uterus shorten to make the uterus smaller, without noticeable contractions and without the mother's having an urge to push. The mother also gets a rest break. Sheila Kitzinger, the well-known British teacher and author, has termed this the "rest and be thankful phase."

How Long Does It Last? The resting phase usually lasts up to twenty or thirty minutes. If it lasts longer than that, most caregivers urge the mother to change position or to push (bear down) in an effort to speed labor along and bring on stronger contractions. They don't want labor to slow down for very long at this point.

What Does the Mother Feel? The start of the birthing stage is always a milestone. The mother will probably welcome this rest, especially after the tumult of transition. She gets "a new lease on life," a second wind. If she was confused, her head is now clear. If she was discouraged, she is now optimistic. If she was withdrawn, she is now outgoing and aware of her surroundings.

Sometimes a women feels anxious if the resting phase seems to go on for too long or if the staff is imploring her to push before she feels an urge to do so. She may also feel inadequate or apologetic if everyone is commanding her to push, making her feel as if she is not doing well enough.

What Does the Caregiver Do? During the resting phase—

- The midwife or nurse remains close by, offering encouragement, praise, and positive suggestions.
- The nurse will probably call the doctor to come now. If the mother has had a child before, the doctor will try to arrive soon after she begins pushing.
- The midwife or nurse may become more directive at this time, telling the mother what positions to try, or how or when to push.
- The midwife or nurse listens frequently to the baby's heartbeat and continues assessing the mother's welfare.
- The midwife or nurse may do a vaginal exam to assess the progress of the baby's descent.

How Can You Help? The birthing stage is an exciting time. Your own feelings about the baby and her imminent birth may overwhelm you. You may be unprepared for how you feel now as you realize you're about to become a parent, or about to see a miracle. Even though you have your own powerful emotional reaction to the birth, you are still the mother's major source of support, so you must remain calm and continue to encourage and assist her. Here are some guidelines:

- Be patient during the resting phase. Don't try to rush the mother through it.
- If the nurse or caregiver wants the mother to push without a contraction or without the urge, ask if she can wait until she feels the urge to push.
- Match her mood. As she leaves the emotions of transition behind, you should do the same.
- Review with the mother and her caregiver what will be happening from now on, as the labor picks up again.

The Descent

What Is It? During the descent phase the uterus contracts strongly again and the mother feels the urge to push. The baby descends through the birth canal to the point where the head is clearly visible. The mother alternately pushes and breathes lightly during contractions and rests between contractions.

The baby's descent is usually intermittent; he moves down when the mother bears down during her urges to push, and slips back during the pauses between the mother's bearing-down efforts. You will find yourself totally engrossed in the moment. You almost hate to see the baby slip back each time because you're so anxious to see him born. You must remember that progress is being made, and this gradual stretching is easier on both baby and mother than constant pressure on the baby's head and continuous stretching of the vagina.

The mother may change positions during the descent phase. The best positions are semisitting, lying on one side, resting on hands and knees, and squatting. Supported squatting and sitting on the toilet are also useful at times. See "Positions for the Birthing (Second) Stage," page 77, which explains the benefits of each of these positions.

How Long Does It Last? The descent phase usually takes up more than half the total time of the birthing stage—from a few minutes to three hours or so.

What Does the Mother Feel? The mother finds strength and determination during the descent phase, even after a long labor. The imminence of the birth heartens her, and she is receptive to suggestions and to praise. She may have other feelings as well:

- She may feel uncertain about what to do and how to do it. She may ask how she is doing, needing reassurance that her sensations are normal, that she is all right.
- She may feel afraid to let go. This is the most difficult thing to do at this time—to let the baby come out. The sensations of descent and of the large solid head stretching the birth canal are gratifying and yet alarming and painful. It is scary to let the baby come *because it hurts*. She may instinctively resist the passage of the baby by tensing her pelvic floor against the baby's downward movement. If the mother did perineal massage during pregnancy, she will now find it easier to relax appropriately. (Prenatal perineal massage is

a rehearsal for the sensations of the birthing stage, and it gives the mother a chance to practice relaxing while her vagina is being stretched. See "Prenatal Perineal Massage," page 16.)

- If the baby's descent is extremely rapid, the mother may feel shocked by the intensity of sensation and by her total lack of control over her body.
- If the descent is very slow, she will become discouraged. This may be the most demanding work of her entire life, and she needs to feel she is making progress.

What Does the Caregiver Do? During the descent phase—

- The nurse or midwife continues as before, encouraging the mother's efforts and reassuring her.
- The doctor usually arrives during this phase, perhaps to your great relief.
- The doctor or midwife performs occasional vaginal exams to confirm the baby's progress. The nurse, midwife, or doctor checks the baby's heart rate and the mother's vital signs periodically.
- The doctor or midwife scrubs and dons surgical gloves, and perhaps special clothing and a mask, when the birth is imminent.
- The nurse, doctor, or midwife may place drapes beneath the mother, may cleanse the mother's vaginal area, and may massage or place hot compresses on the perineum.
- The doctor or midwife uses his or her hands to control the emergence of the baby's head.

How Can You Help? With so many people around during the descent phase, you may feel less vital to the mother than you felt earlier. It is true that she now receives much of her direction and praise from others. This may be a relief to you because it allows you to become absorbed in your own experience of the birth. You are, however, still the mother's birth partner—the one who has seen her through all this—and she still may rely on you despite all of the attention from others. Here are some suggestions:

- Stay close to the mother, where she can see, feel, and hear you. You may support her from behind or by her side.
- Compliment her; tell her how well she is doing—with every contraction.
- Stay calm. Try to maintain a steady and reassuring tone of voice and a confident, firm touch (don't rub her or squeeze her too hard in your excitement); continue to encourage her.

- See if the mother is relaxing her perineum during bearing-down efforts. You may be able to tell if you can see her anus. If her perineum is relaxed, her anus will bulge open as she bears down. If it is tense, her anus constricts or appears tight.
- If she is not relaxing her perineum, remind her to let go, open up, let the baby out. Use whatever suggestions will help her release the tension in her perineum. Remind her to relax as she did during perineal massage (page 16). Request warm compresses to place on her perineum.
- Remind the mother that the baby is almost here!
- If progress is slow, suggest that she try a different position. See "Positions for the Birthing (Second) Stage," page 77, which explains the benefits of each of these positions.
- Remember that during a few contractions after the baby's head becomes visible at the vaginal opening, it may appear abnormal—wrinkled and spongy. Pressure on the head by the vaginal wall causes the skin of the scalp to be squeezed up to the top of the head (one birth partner thought it was a brain without a scalp!) until the head moves down more. Then it looks more as you would expect—hard and smooth.

Few people are prepared for the power of the moment: the mother's superhuman effort; the sounds she makes; the baby bulging the vagina, peeking its wet and wrinkled scalp out, only to retreat yet again; the charged atmosphere of the room as everyone anticipates the birth. It is impossible to describe the awe, excitement, and tension you will feel as you await the moment of birth. However, don't forget that the mother still needs your support and attention.

The Crowning and Birth Phase

What Is It? The crowning and birth phase is when the baby is actually born. It is the transition from the birthing to the placental stage. It begins when the baby's head crowns—that is, when it remains visible at the vaginal opening even between contractions, no longer sneaking back between the mother's bearing-down efforts. This phase ends when the baby is born.

During the crowning and birth phase the mother's vagina and perineum are stretched more than at any other time and they are more likely to sustain damage at this time than during any other phase. Protecting the perineum now becomes a major focus of the caregiver's management.

Until now, the baby's head has appeared wrinkled and spongy.

Once the head crowns, the skin evens out over the scalp. The head seems to lurch forward a few times, and then it emerges—top of the head, brow and ears, then the face. The head rotates to one side, one shoulder appears, and the rest of the baby slides out with a gush of water.

At first the baby appears blue and lifeless, but within seconds he begins breathing, usually with a gurgle, then a lusty cry. Immediately, the baby begins to turn more pink, and very soon he will be a healthy pink or ruddy color.

How Long Does It Last? The crowning and birth phase takes only a few contractions.

What Does the Mother Feel? The mother's body gives mixed messages during the crowning and birth phase: On the one hand, she knows the baby is almost here and she is anxious to push hard to get him or her out quickly. On the other hand, she feels the stretching and burning (the "rim of fire") that signal her to stop pushing. To prevent the vagina or perineum from tearing, she should heed the message to stop pushing and ease the baby out, *not* to push hard.

Although the crowning and birth are exciting for everyone else, this phase may be acutely painful for the mother, who has to devote all of her attention to getting the baby out. After the head has emerged, she still needs to carefully give birth to the shoulders; the body then comes on its own.

Some mothers touch the baby's head or body as it emerges. The mother may glow with joy or withdraw her hand in surprise if it doesn't feel the way she expected it to.

After the birth, it may take her a few moments to realize that labor is over (or nearly so), and to shift her attention to the baby. This takes longer for some women than others.

What Does the Caregiver Do? During the crowning and birth phase, the caregiver—

• Supports the perineum and controls the passage of the head as it crowns.
• Asks the mother to stop pushing as the head emerges. In fact, the mother should stop pushing whenever she begins to feel the burning and stretching. To do this, the mother raises her chin and blows lightly throughout the contraction. (See "Avoiding Pushing," page 89.) The uterus will still contract and give the mother an urge

to push, but the mother can keep from holding her breath and straining.

- Decides if it is necessary to perform an episiotomy (see "Episiotomy," page 138).
- Holds the baby's head as it emerges and may encourage both you and the mother to touch the baby or even hold her body as she comes out.
- Dries the baby and places her on the mother's abdomen where the mother can hold her, or in a heated crib nearby. A nurse or doctor checks the baby quickly and gives her an Apgar score (see page 125) when she is one minute old and again when she is five minutes old. Five signs are evaluated in order to decide if the baby needs extra immediate care, close observation, or no extra attention at all. A total score of seven points or above is very good. If the score is below 7, at both one and five minutes, the baby needs extra observation and care until the problems are corrected.

How Can You Help? During the crowning and birth phase, you can help the mother in the following ways:

- Stay close by.
- If the mother is overly anxious to push the baby out and wants to push hard, give her very firm guidance to help her stop pushing so that she will not injure herself or the baby with an unduly rapid delivery.
- Help her avoid pushing by getting her to follow your verbal directions: "Raise your chin, look at me, blow . . . , blow . . . that's the way . . . blow . . . ," and so forth.
- Help her interpret the caregiver's directions if she is unsure about what to do.
- Remind her to look in the mirror (to see the baby's head crown and to see the baby being born) and to touch the baby's head, especially if she has said earlier that she wants to do these things.
- Participate in this miracle in the way that is most comfortable for you. Stay at the mother's head and focus on her if you feel squeamish about watching the baby come out. Or, take it all in by watching in the mirror or by moving so that you can watch closely. Please, though, don't get so caught up in the birth that you ignore the mother!
- Remember that although the baby's initial appearance is dusky (bluish) and almost lifeless, it will begin to change within seconds as the baby breathes and cries.

The Placental Stage

What Is It? The placental stage begins when the baby is born and ends after the placenta (sometimes called the afterbirth) is born.

This stage is usually anticlimactic when compared with the baby's birth, and many women barely notice their few contractions and the emergence of the placenta. The two phases of the placental stage, the separation of the placenta and the expulsion of the placenta, are usually imperceptible to the mother. Medical professionals call this the *third stage* of labor.

How Long Does It Last? The placental stage is the shortest stage of labor. It usually lasts only fifteen to thirty minutes.

What Does the Mother Feel? A flood of deep emotions sweeps over the mother during the placental stage. The apparent end of labor, the new baby, the rest of the job to be done—all vie for her attention.

- The mother may find the birth of the placenta interesting and fascinating, or she may devote all of her attention to the baby and you, hardly noticing when the placenta comes out.
- For a few minutes she may be unable to feel anything except relief that her ordeal is over: the pushing, the pain, the contractions have stopped.
- She may marvel at her new shape and her very soft abdomen.
- She may become preoccupied with the baby or with establishing suckling at the breast.
- She may begin to tremble all over and to feel weak.

What Does the Caregiver Do? During the placental stage the caregiver—

- Attends to the umbilical cord, clamping it and cutting it. Sometimes the caregiver withdraws a sample of blood from the cord (for example, to analyze for the baby's blood type).
- Dries and checks the baby.
- Checks the mother's birth canal for tears.
- Attends to the placenta. When the placenta has separated from the uterine wall (the caregiver can tell by feeling the uterus and pulling gently on the cord), he or she may ask the mother to push gently to deliver the placenta.
- Carefully inspects the placenta to be sure that all of it was delivered.

How Can You Help? During the placental stage you can do the following:

- Cut the cord, if you want to. The symbolism of separating mother and baby appeals to some women and their partners. The cord is very firm and slippery. When you cut it, don't snip gently. It takes a decisive effort.
- Enjoy the baby and help the mother to do the same—that is your main role now. Make sure the mother is comfortable, that she can see the baby, and that she is warm enough.
- Make sure the baby stays warm. Cover her with warm blankets; don't unwrap her; keep her head covered. If a newborn is chilled, she can take a long time to regain her temperature.
- Go along if the baby has to be removed to the nursery (either because of a health problem or because it is hospital policy), unless the mother needs you to remain with her.
- Take advantage of any chance you have to hold the baby close; talk to the baby and begin getting acquainted.
- Congratulate yourselves on a job well done, and begin making those phone calls, as the after-birth care (page 191) of mother and baby begins.

Normal Labor—in a Nutshell

The table on page 70–72 summarizes the events in normal labor and the ways you can help. You may find this table useful as a quick reference during labor.

NORMAL LABOR—IN A NUTSHELL

Stage/Phase of Labor	What Happens	How You Can Help
PRELABOR (off-and-on or constant for hours or days)	• Cervix softens, thins. • Mother has some possible or preliminary signs of labor (page 38), or both. • Mother may become anxious or tired if it lasts a long time.	• Encourage normal activities in the daytime, as long as they are not strenuous; rest at night. • Distracting activities are appropriate. • Mother should eat whenever she feels like it. • Time contractions off and on. Use the "Early Labor Record" (page 45). • Be patient; do not get over-excited or preoccupied with contractions. • Mother can bathe or shower to relax.
DILATION (FIRST) STAGE (2 to 24 hours)		
Early labor (a few hours to 20 hours)	• Cervix continues thinning, opens to about 4 or 5 cm. • Mother has one or both positive signs of labor (page 39)—progress usually begins slowly.	• Continue as in prelabor. • Suggest slow breathing and relaxation when mother cannot walk or talk through contractions without pausing. • If bag of waters breaks, take precautions (page 37); call caregiver. • Remain with the mother.
Active labor (½ hour to 6 hours)	• Cervix dilates from about 5 to 8 cm. • Contractions become intense or painful; last 60 seconds or more; come closer—every 5 or fewer minutes. • Progress speeds up. • Mother may feel trapped, discouraged; becomes quiet, serious, focused on her labor.	• Go to the hospital, or make sure the midwife is on her way, if she hasn't arrived yet. • Present the mother's Birth Plan to the nurse or midwife (page 20). • Give mother your total, undivided attention for every contraction. • Match her quiet, serious, focused mood. • Encourage her. Point out the more rapid progress. • Use comfort measures (page 73). For backache, use cold or heat, counterpressure, positions (page 109). Use the Take-Charge Routine if necessary (page 94). • If you are worried or uncertain, ask staff or caregiver for help, explanations, reassurance.

70

Stage/Phase of Labor	What Happens	How You Can Help
Active labor— *continued*		• Offer a sip of liquid after each contraction. • Remind her to urinate every hour or two.
Transition phase (10 to 60 minutes)	• Cervix dilates from about 8 cm to complete (10 cm); usually lasts 5 to 20 contractions. • Mother has very long, painful contractions, with little break between. • Baby may begin descent, giving mother pressure in rectum, possible urge to push. • Mother becomes restless, tense, overwhelmed, irritable, despairing. She may weep, cry out, want to give up or fight contractions. She may doze the few seconds between contractions. • Mother may tremble, vomit; her skin may hurt when rubbed.	• Continue as much as possible as in the active phase. • Stay very close. • Focus on one contraction at a time. • Let mother doze or relax between contractions. It is okay if she does not relax *during* these contractions. • Remind mother that transition is short, that she is almost ready to begin pushing her baby out. • Use Take-Charge Routine (page 94); talk her through contractions, if necessary. • Firm touch usually helps; rubbing may be annoying. • Call nurse or caregiver if mother begins pushing. • Help her push or keep from pushing (page 59) according to findings of vaginal exam.
BIRTHING (SECOND) STAGE (15 minutes to over 3 hours)		
Resting phase (0 to 20 minutes)	• Cervix is fully dilated. • Contractions may subside or seem to stop for 15 to 20 minutes. • Uterus is "collecting itself" for upcoming effort. • Resting phase may not occur if baby is very low. • Mother becomes clear-headed, optimistic, and determined; may wonder why labor "stopped." • Staff may want mother to begin pushing even without contractions.	• Be patient; remind mother of the lull of the resting phase. • If staff tells mother to push without the urge, ask if she can wait for urge to push. • Encourage mother to relax and take advantage of the rest. • If 20 minutes pass without pushing contractions, suggest that mother change position (try hands and knees, squat, or supported squat, page 77).
Descent phase (10 minutes to 2½ hours)	• Baby moves down the birth canal. • Strong contractions resume. • The urge to push becomes stronger and more frequent with each contraction.	• Remind mother to relax her pelvic floor: say, for example, "Open up"; "Let the baby come." • Encourage mother to bear down and push when she feels the urge.

NORMAL LABOR—IN A NUTSHELL

Stage/Phase of Labor	What Happens	How You Can Help
Descent phase —*continued*	• Mother cannot avoid pushing. The urge is strong and involuntary. It comes from inside; she cannot make it happen. • Mother may be alarmed at feeling the baby's head in vagina. She may resist its passage by tensing her pelvic floor. • Baby moves down during each pushing effort, slips back between pushes.	• Suggest that mother sit on toilet for a few contractions if she is resisting passage of baby. • Hot compresses may help relax the perineum. • Reinforce her efforts. Tell her how well she is doing. • Suggest that she touch baby's head; she may or may not like what she feels. • Baby's head appears wrinkled; do not be alarmed. • Help mother change positions (page 65) if she needs to.
Crowning and birth phase (2 to 20 minutes)	• Baby's head no longer slips back between pushes. • Birth of head is imminent (within a few contractions). • Mother feels intense burning, stinging in vagina ("rim of fire"). She may be confused, wanting to push very hard to get the baby out right away but feeling she may split if she pushes. • Baby's head emerges, rotates; then the shoulders and the rest of the body are born.	• Don't rush mother; remind her to *stop pushing* and "breathe her baby out," or pant (with her chin up) to keep from pushing (page 67). • Help her tune in to caregiver's instructions. • Help mother hold baby, preferably skin to skin. • Baby must be kept warm. Cover with warm blankets.
PLACENTAL (THIRD) STAGE (5 to 30 minutes)	• Mother may be very shaky. • Uterus cramps. • Placenta separates from wall of uterus. • Cord is clamped and cut. • Birth of placenta is often hardly noticed.	• Enjoy baby. • You may want to cut cord. • Make sure mother and baby are warm and comfortable. • You may want to hold baby if mother is not ready or has pain during contractions or stitching.

72

4

Comfort Measures for Labor

There are numerous techniques for reducing pain in labor. They do not take away *all* pain, but when combined with caring and skilled labor support, these techniques enable many women to cope successfully with their pain—to keep it manageable. Some women use these techniques in combination with pain-relieving medications; others rely totally on the techniques.

Be sure, before labor begins, that you know and respect the mother's preferences regarding her use of pain medications. Use the "Pain Medications Preference Scale," page 163, to help you find out how she feels and whether your feelings are different from hers. Then you will know how to react if and when she approaches the limits of her tolerance of pain. You will either (1) ask for pain medication (see "Medications for Pain during Labor," page 161), or (2) redouble your efforts in encouraging, guiding, and helping the mother to continue handling her pain. For the latter, you will find many of the comfort measures described here to be highly effective.

The techniques described in this chapter work in any of three different ways:

1. By actually addressing and reducing the pain at its source.
2. By increasing other pleasant or neutral sensations to dampen the mother's awareness of the pain.

3. By involving her in activities that focus her attention on something besides the pain.

Learn about the following techniques before labor begins so that you will be better prepared to help the mother use them. Alternating among a variety of techniques seems more helpful than doing the same thing for the entire labor. Use the information in this chapter and the lists in chapter 1 to pack a bag of comfort items to take to the hospital with you (or to have ready in your home) to use during labor.

Spontaneous Rituals

Most couples develop their own "rituals" for handling the mother's contractions; that is, they repeat the same series of comforting actions with each contraction. Although the rituals change from time to time and are occasionally interrupted by care-giving tasks, new people arriving, or the telephone ringing, women come to rely on them in active labor to get them through. These rituals cannot really be planned in advance; they emerge *during* labor. They usually include some of the "tried and true" comfort measures, like patterned breathing and attention focusing, included in this chapter, along with individual variations and additions that suit the mother's needs at the time.

Here are some guidelines for developing and using rituals:

1. Begin to use a ritual when the contractions demand the mother's attention—when she cannot walk or talk through them without pausing.

2. As a basic ritual, use relaxation and patterned breathing and attention focusing (pages 83–90).

3. Add any comfort measures from this chapter that help the mother. Adapt the comfort measures to suit the mother's preferences. This involves some trial and error.

4. Add other personal touches you can think of (certain words, ways of touching her) that might be soothing to her. (The examples that follow show how some couples have done this.)

5. Once you figure out what helps most, repeat the ritual for many contractions in a row. When the effectiveness of one ritual diminishes, change it, add to it, or try something completely different.

6. You may find that if there are constant interruptions—nurses or caregivers examining her, checking her pulse, taking her temper-

ature or blood pressure, drawing blood, monitoring her, and so forth, the mother may be unable to find a ritual. If she finds interventions to be unsettling, you might say, "If we could try a few without interruption, I think she could get back on top of these contractions. Is this possible?" If the procedures cannot be postponed, you may need to play a more active "coaching" role (see "The Take-Charge Routine," page 94) until the mother can have some quiet, undisturbed time to develop her ritual.

The following examples describe rituals developed by some women and their birth partners. You can see how people add their personal touches to get the most out of the comfort measures.

One couple found themselves handling the contractions by having the birth partner (her husband) scratch the mother's back during each contraction while she knelt on the floor and leaned forward onto his lap. The mother had always loved having her back scratched, and found that during contractions it really helped if he scratched it lightly, moving gradually upward from the left buttock to the left shoulder, over to the right shoulder, and down to the right buttock. Following the changes in her breathing, he timed it so that when he reached her right shoulder the contraction had peaked, and when he reached her right buttock it had ended. This back scratching was a helpful focus for the mother; she knew where she was in the contraction by where her birth partner was scratching! Other birth partners have helped the mother know when the contraction has passed the halfway point by counting breaths, calling off ten- or fifteen-second intervals during each contraction, or watching the fetal monitor for signs that the contraction is fading.

In another case, the ritual involved hair brushing. The laboring woman had long, straight, silky hair, and she found that she could cope well as long as her mother brushed it during the contractions. If her mother stopped, the woman felt more pain. It happened that her mother had often brushed the woman's hair when she was a child and teenager and during those times they had felt very close to each other. The daughter had felt safe and content then, and these same feelings surfaced during her labor.

The development of rituals is a truly creative aspect of labor, although it is largely unrecognized by caregivers and by childbirth educators and authors. It is not comfort measures by themselves that reduce pain; rather it is the mother's unique adaptation of these measures to suit her personality and her needs at the time.

Movement and Position Changes

When the mother is free to move and change positions, she is more comfortable and her labor may even speed up. Every twenty to thirty minutes during the dilation stage, remind her to try standing; walking; sitting; semireclining; squatting; kneeling; lying on her side; getting on her hands and knees; or leaning on the birth partner, the wall, the bed, or the nightstand. Don't insist that she change position, however, especially when she is coping well and is making good progress.

Some women use a series of positions with each contraction: for example, sitting or walking between contractions, then standing up and leaning on their birth partner during contractions. (See "Backache in Labor," page 109, for further discussion of the use of positions during the dilation stage.)

During the birthing stage, too, especially if it takes more than an hour, the mother may use several different positions. Just before the actual birth of the baby, the caregiver may ask her to assume a position that he or she prefers (such as semisitting). See the table "Positions for the Birthing (Second) Stage" for a list of useful positions and the possible benefits of each.

Counterpressure

If the mother has backache—

- Press your fist, the heel of your hand, or a firm object (a tennis ball, a rolling pin, a cold can of soda pop, or an ice pack) against her low back during contractions.
- Hold on to the front of her hip as you press, because she may want you to press so hard that you would push her over otherwise!
- Try pressing in different spots; she will tell you where it feels best.
- See "Backache in Labor," page 109, for other comfort measures for backache.

Baths, Showers, and Whirlpool Baths

Until recently, baths and showers were rarely used by laboring women. They may be as good as, or even better than, narcotics at relieving pain and tension, and they don't have any side effects. Immersion in water is relaxing, and the buoyancy reduces the pain of contractions.

POSITIONS FOR THE BIRTHING (SECOND) STAGE

Position	Possible benefits	Comments
Semisitting, with or without legs pulled up	• Good resting position (if legs are not pulled up) • Uses gravity somewhat to bring the baby down • Pulling legs up sometimes helps the baby descend • Easy position on a bed or delivery table, and a favorite of most caregivers	
Sidelying	• Good resting position • Helps slow a rapid delivery • Takes pressure off hemorrhoids • Takes pressure off mother's sacrum and coccyx, allowing them to move back slightly and enlarge the space within her pelvis • Preferable for women with high blood pressure	
Resting on hands and knees, or kneeling and leaning forward with support	• May relieve backache • Helps rotate baby to the most favorable (OA, or occiput anterior) position • May correct slowing of baby's heart rate • Takes pressure off hemorrhoids	
Sitting on the toilet	• By drawing on mother's associations with moving her bowels, may help her relax her pelvic floor and improve her effectiveness in pushing • Uses gravity	• Recommended, for a few contractions, only if mother is not pushing effectively and only until the crowning phase, when she feels burning and stinging (*She does not give birth while sitting on the toilet!*)
Squatting on bed or floor, using a squatting bar, human support, or other aid, if necessary	• Uses gravity • Spreads the pelvic bones, giving more room than any other position • Requires less bearing-down effort	

POSITIONS FOR THE BIRTHING (SECOND) STAGE—*Continued*

Position	Possible benefits	Comments
Squatting—*continued*	• In a difficult birth, may help baby rotate and descend • Helpful if mother does not feel an urge to push	Not recommended in a very rapid second (birth) stage
Supported squat during contractions: mother stands and leans back against birth partner, lowering herself as he or she supports her weight under the arms	• Eliminates all external pressures on pelvis and relaxes muscles attached to pelvis, allowing descending baby to ease through • In a difficult birth, may help baby rotate and descend • Uses gravity	Hard work for the birth partner, who may be able to do this for only a few contractions

The skin stimulation provided by a shower or whirlpool (Jacuzzi) is pleasant and effective in counteracting the awareness of pain.

Encourage the mother to relax in a warm (not hot) bath, with or without whirlpool, or in a shower. If there is a hand-held shower head, direct it either on her abdomen or low back. It can be a godsend. Most caregivers advise the mother not to take a tub bath if her bag of waters has broken; showers are still fine. See "If the Bag of Waters Breaks before Labor Begins," page 37.

The mother's contractions will seem less intense in the bath or shower, and in prolonged early labor she is more likely to rest thoroughly or even to sleep in the tub than out of it. Baths sometimes speed progress in slow labors.

Heat and Cold

Heat and cold can be used at any time during labor and afterwards to relieve a number of discomforts:

• Place a hot water bottle, a hot damp towel, or an electric heating pad on the mother's low abdomen, back, or groin to ease pain during the dilation (first) stage.
• Use a warm blanket to relieve trembling during the transition phase.
• Use hot compresses on the perineum (area between her vagina and

Positions for laboring out of bed.

anus) during the birthing stage to relieve pain and to help her relax her birth canal.

- Use a cool damp washcloth to wipe the mother's brow and face between contractions.
- Use an ice bag, a rubber glove filled with crushed ice, frozen wet washcloths, or a bag of frozen peas to relieve low back pain. Or roll an ice-filled, hollow plastic rolling pin (made by Tupperware); a can of frozen juice; or a frozen, rounded plastic bottle of water over her back.
- Use cold packs to relieve pain from hemorrhoids or stitches after the birth.

Caution: Be careful not to make the packs so hot or so cold that you cause burns or frost damage to the mother's skin. The rule is: If you can't hold it in your hands, don't put it on her. Let the hot pack cool, or put layers of towels between her skin and the hot or cold pack to protect her, if necessary.

Transcutaneous Electrical Nerve Stimulation (TENS)

TENS has been used successfully for years to treat postoperative and chronic pain. It is now also becoming popular for childbirth and postcesarean pain. Because TENS is still unknown to many obstetric caregivers, you may have to suggest it yourself if you are interested. The mother's caregiver can obtain more information about TENS from a physical therapist. A TENS unit is available for rent from the hospital physical therapy department or from medical-supply rental companies.

The TENS unit consists of four flexible, Band-Aid–size pads connected by wires to a small (cassette tape–size) battery-operated generator of electric impulses. The pads adhere to the mother's skin alongside her low spine. You or she can regulate the impulses. During a contraction you turn on the current by turning up two dials until she feels a vibration, tingling, or prickling—just enough to diminish her awareness of the pain. When the contraction ends, you turn down the current so that she feels nothing.

Consult her caregiver if the mother wants to try TENS or to learn more about it. A physical therapist can show both of you how to use the TENS unit.

Many women who have used TENS during labor swear it enabled them to avoid using pain-relieving medication; others report it was

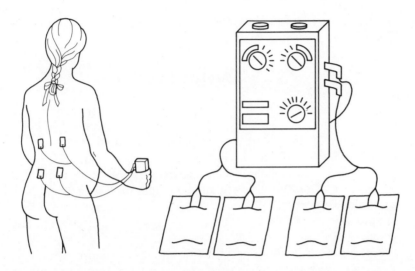

*A transcutaneous electrical nerve stimulation (TENS) unit (*right*), and the device in use (* left*).*

helpful in diminishing their pain; still others say it did little good. As for safety, no adverse effects have been reported, except that TENS sometimes interferes with output from the electronic fetal monitor. Further studies of both the safety and the effectiveness of TENS are desirable.

Touch and Massage

Touch conveys a kind, caring, and comforting message to the laboring mother. Find out what kind of touch the mother finds soothing and try it during labor. She will appreciate a gentle, comforting gesture —rubbing of a painful spot, a reassuring pat, a tight embrace, stroking of her hair or cheek. Or, she may prefer a more formal massage—a rhythmic rubbing or kneading of her back, legs, shoulders, and so forth. Use oil or cornstarch on your hands so they won't stick to and irritate the mother's skin.

Try a very light massage (with the fingertips only) on the mother's abdomen during contractions (this is sometimes called *effleurage*). You can also use this light massage on her thighs or elsewhere if she finds it more relaxing than a firm massage. The mother may find rubbing and stroking wonderful during early labor but intolerable during transition. If so, try holding her head or shoulders, hand, foot, or thigh firmly—without rubbing.

Acupressure

Shiatsu, or acupressure, has been practiced in the Orient for many centuries. This healing art is derived from the ancient Chinese understanding of the principles of *yin* and *yang*. The body is made up of twelve meridians, along which vital forces flow; acupressure corrects imbalances in the flow of these vital forces. Although these ideas differ greatly from Western scientific thought, the use of acupressure has gained interest in the West. Many people successfully combine acupressure with other methods to provide comfort and promote progress in labor.

By pressing with your finger or thumb at certain acupressure points, you may be able to relieve the mother's pain and speed up her labor. The two most popular points for labor are the Ho-ku point and Spleen 6. Both are sensitive spots that may hurt when you apply acupressure properly.

The Ho-ku point is on the back of the hand, where the bones forming the bases of the thumb and index finger come together. Press steadily into the bone at the base of the index finger with your thumb for ten to fifteen seconds, three times, with a brief rest in between. You can repeat this as often as you and the mother want.

Spleen 6 is on the inner side of the lower leg about four finger breadths above the ankle. Press your thumb into the bone from slightly behind it for about a minute at a time, or ten to fifteen seconds at a

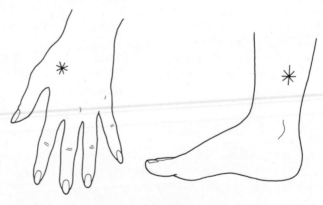

The Ho-ku point (left) *and Spleen 6 (* right).

time, three times, with a brief rest in between. You can repeat this whenever you and the mother want.

Caution: Experts advise against pressing these points on a pregnant woman before her due date as they can cause contractions as well as reduce pain. Find them on yourself but don't use them on the mother until the need arises.

Hypnosis

Many laboring women can achieve a trance state during which they are able to remain relaxed, with a reduced awareness of the pain. The use of hypnosis during labor requires *proper training in advance.* The hypnotic trance can be induced by the mother herself, by a trained birth partner, or by a hypnotherapist who accompanies the mother during labor.

Relaxation

Relaxation, patterned breathing, and attention-focusing have long been the cornerstones of childbirth preparation. Of these three, relaxation is the most important; it is the goal of most comfort measures. If a woman lets her body go limp during her contractions, she will feel less pain. The mother's attempt to relax, even if not completely successful, is helpful in itself because it serves as a positive focus away from her pain.

During the last weeks of pregnancy, help the mother learn to recognize and release tension in all parts of her body. By practicing with her, you can learn what tone of voice, which words, and what sort of touch help her relax. Try the following:

1. While she lies still, tell the mother which parts to focus on and relax. Start at her toes, and gradually go through her body parts to her head.

2. Help her to relax during activity—to relax parts of her body, that is, while others are tense or working. For example, you can tell her to relax her shoulders while eating, her brow while watching TV. With your help she may become more aware of her tension and learn to relax those parts not needed for a particular activity.

3. If she has a "tension spot"—a part of her body where tension seems to settle—help her identify that part and let go of tension there when you touch the spot or when you say, for example, "Relax your

right shoulder." Her tension spot might be in her shoulders, neck, brow, jaw, or low back. This same spot is likely to be the seat of tension during labor. If the mother has difficulty relaxing, she can learn to let a particular part of her body go limp by first tensing it (tightening the muscles as much as possible) and then relaxing it. Repeating this exercise trains the mother to recognize when her body is tense and to relax it.

Good childbirth preparation classes emphasize relaxation techniques. Audio tapes are also available to help people master the art of relaxation. See "Recommended Resources" for a description of a tape that I have made for pregnant women.

During labor you can help the mother to relax in the following ways:

1. When she feels a contraction begin, remind her to take a long, deep sigh and release the tension everywhere as she breathes out.

2. If she tenses in any parts of her body as the contraction intensifies, remind her with soothing words and touch to let go of the tension in those places. Don't just say, "Relax." She needs you to be more specific than that. Instead say, "Let go right here," as you touch her hands, brow, shoulders, and so forth.

3. Use the comfort measures in this chapter and verbal reminders to help the mother relax during and between contractions. Trial and error will tell you what works best. Once you find something that works, stick with it.

4. If labor is so intense that the mother is unable to relax *during* contractions despite your efforts, then help her relax and rest *between* contractions. Use soothing words, touch, and other comfort measures.

Attention Focusing

This technique diverts the mother's mind from her pain by having her concentrate on something else. During contractions the mother can focus her attention in one of several ways:

1. She can *look* at you or at something else.

2. She can *listen* to your voice, to music, or to another soothing sound.

3. She can *focus* on your touch, your massage, or your caress.

4. She can *concentrate* on a mental drill such as counting or repeating words to herself throughout each contraction (for example: she might chant "ooopen, . . . ooopen, . . . ooopen, . . ."; repeat "I

think I can, . . . I think I can, . . . I thought I could, . . . I thought I could, . . . (from the book *The Little Engine That Could*) or count down from 100 during each contraction.

Visualization

The mother can visualize something positive, pleasant, or relaxing, using her contractions, her focus, or her breathing as a cue. For example, she might visualize her exhalations or your soothing touch or massage as drawing her tension and pain away. She might visualize each contraction in various ways: as a wave, with herself floating over the crest; or as a mountain, which she climbs up and down as the contractions come and go. She might use the onset of the contraction as a cue to imagine herself soaring like a seagull above the waves of contractions below. Several women from my childbirth classes have told me that during labor they visualized the opening of the cervix of my knitted argyle uterus, which I used to demonstrate contractions and dilation during classes. Some visualizations are planned; others emerge spontaneously. They are usually very creative and personally helpful.

Patterned Breathing

Breathing patterns, along with relaxation, have represented the mainstay of childbirth preparation since its inception. Although some childbirth educators have abandoned patterned breathing because it keeps the mother from behaving spontaneously during labor, I think it has tremendous value because it offers the following unique pain-relieving capabilities:

- Patterned breathing helps the mother relax, especially when she has learned and practiced the various patterns in advance.
- Patterned breathing, with its steady rhythm, is calming, especially when labor is in turmoil.
- Patterned breathing may give the mother a sense of well-being, letting her know she has some measure of control over her own behavior, even though her uterus, with its involuntary and all-encompassing contractions, is completely outside her conscious control.
- When institutional policies or the woman's own condition do not permit a wide range of behavior, patterned breathing is always

available as an effective comfort measure. For example, the mother may not be able to use some of the other comfort measures, such as baths or showers and movement, because (1) she cannot get out of bed, (2) an electronic monitor or intravenous line is in the way, or (3) she has received medications that make using these comfort measures impossible. See "If the Mother Must Labor in Bed," page 111, for specific suggestions for such circumstances.

The mother should learn and practice the various breathing patterns before labor so that she will be able to use them most effectively and with the least effort during labor—when she will really need them.

Breathing Patterns for Labor

There are three basic breathing patterns for the dilation (first) stage: slow, light (or accelerated), and "pant-pant-blow" (or transition). Until recently, all childbirth educators who taught breathing patterns said they should be used in this order during labor: first slow, then light, then "pant-pant-blow." This teaching does not take into account the preferences of individual women. I suggest that you and the mother learn each of the breathing patterns, adapt their speed and rhythm so you feel comfortable with them, and then use them in any order you like during labor. The mother's preferences and the nature of the contractions should guide the two of you in deciding how and in what order to use the patterns.

Because it is easiest and most relaxing, I usually suggest beginning with slow breathing. Start when the contractions reach a level of intensity where the mother cannot continue walking, or talking, or whatever she is doing, right through the contraction—in other words, when she has to pause until the contraction eases. From then on she should use one of the three breathing patterns with each contraction. She should continue the slow breathing for as long as she can relax well with it. She should switch to another pattern (light or "pant-pant-blow") when the slow breathing is no longer helpful. Then, if her second pattern becomes ineffective, she should switch to the other remaining pattern.

Slow Breathing. Slow breathing is very relaxing and calming. The key is that the mother breathe easily and not work too hard to keep it slow: easy in, easy out. You can tell if she's working too hard at it because her breathing will sound tense and strained. This is how to use slow breathing during labor:

1. When the contraction begins, the mother focuses her attention, as described on page 84.

2. She takes a big, relaxing sigh (the "cleansing" or "greeting" breath), releasing tension throughout her body as she breathes out.

3. She breathes slowly in through her nose and—preferably, though not absolutely necessarily—out through her mouth, in long breaths, with each out-breath sounding like a sigh. The rate is somewhere between five and twelve breaths a minute.

4. As the contraction ends, she takes another big sigh—the "good-bye" breath.

5. She thinks of each breath out as a relaxing breath.

The mother should begin with slow breathing and use it for as long as it continues to help her relax. For some women, slow breathing is all they need throughout labor; others use it until the cervix opens to about eight centimeters (transition phase); others, with very intense, close contractions, may have to switch to light or "pant-pant-blow" (transition) breathing earlier. If the mother switches to light breathing early in labor, she might be able to return to slow breathing after a while. Suggest it, because the slow breathing is restful and the others may be tiring.

Light (Accelerated) Breathing. The light breathing pattern is tricky because it is an artificial pattern. It takes time to learn, just as it takes time to learn to breathe rhythmically while swimming the crawl stroke. And, just as rhythmic breathing when swimming enables one to swim better, the light breathing pattern enables the mother to better manage pain. This is how to use light breathing during labor:

1. When the contraction begins, the mother focuses her attention.

2. She takes a big, relaxing sigh.

3. She begins breathing in the slow pattern, shortening and lightening her breaths as the contraction intensifies.

4. At the peak of the contraction, she is breathing lightly through her mouth (with a silent in-breath, and a blowing sound emphasizing the out-breath) at a rate of 30 to 120 breaths per minute.

5. The mother continues at this rate until the contraction begins to subside. Then she gradually slows down the breathing rate until the contraction is over.

6. The contraction ends. She takes another big sigh.

Please encourage the mother to practice this pattern enough to master it. It doesn't take more than a few practice sessions. At first light breathing is uncomfortable (it may cause dry mouth, light-headedness, or a feeling that she can't get enough air), but by adapting it and working with it, she can learn to remain relaxed and comfortable while doing it. Light breathing may become her best friend in labor (besides you).

Practice this pattern until the mother is able to do the peak rate of 30 to 120 breaths per minute for a full one and a half to two minutes without stopping or feeling lightheaded (from hyperventilating). If she feels lightheaded, have her slow her pace slightly or breathe more shallowly. The lightheadedness is harmless, although it is annoying and uncomfortable; it will not occur once she masters the technique. See that the mother relaxes all over, especially in the shoulders and trunk, as she practices this pattern. If she is tense, she is more likely to hyperventilate. Remind her to relax. Coach the mother by breathing with her or by using your hand to "conduct" her breathing. Keep your hand and wrist relaxed and floppy while conducting. Your own relaxation is contagious and will help her relax.

"Pant-Pant-Blow" (Transition) Breathing. "Pant-pant-blow," or transition breathing, is almost a combination of the slow and light patterns. Most women use slow breathing first, switch to light breathing, and then switch to "pant-pant-blow." Others use "pant-pant-blow" second and light breathing third. It is a matter of personal preference.

This is how to use "pant-pant-blow" breathing during labor:

1. When the contraction begins, the mother focuses her attention.
2. She takes a big, relaxing sigh.
3. Through her mouth, she takes three or four short, light breaths in and out, followed by a *long*, relaxing breath out. In other words three or four panting breaths are followed by a blowing breath. She emphasizes each out-breath, making it audible. In-breaths are silent.
4. She repeats this short-short-short-short-long pattern until the end of the contraction, when she takes another big sigh.

Under some circumstances you might want the mother to vary the number of short breaths per long breath within the contraction. Hold up a number of fingers, meaning that she should take that number of pants or light breaths before the next blow or long out-breath. Then after the blow, hold up a different number of fingers. The mother follows the directions you give. This "scramble" breathing helps women who want or need some distraction late in labor.

Feel free to adapt these breathing patterns to make the mother as comfortable as possible. Do remember, however, that the benefit comes from having familiar patterns that the mother can do easily— without thinking much about it, without discomfort, and without tensing. These patterns should be relaxing; they become good attention-focusing aids in themselves once the mother has practiced them.

Breathing Patterns for Pushing (Bearing-Down Techniques)

There are three techniques for handling the urge to push: one is used to *avoid pushing* (or bearing down) when this would be counterproductive. The other two are used during the birthing stage, when the mother *should* be pushing; they are *spontaneous bearing down* and *directed pushing*.

Avoiding Pushing. There are two occasions during labor when the mother might feel like pushing (holding her breath and straining) but should not do so:

- During transition she may have a strong urge to push while there is still a firm lip, or rim, of cervix remaining. Pushing might cause swelling of the cervix from the increased pressure of the baby against it, thus slowing the progress of labor. She should not push until the lip has disappeared. (See "The Transition Phase," page 57.)
- During the birthing stage, as the baby's head crowns and emerges, pushing hard might cause rapid delivery and injury to the mother's vagina.

To help the mother avoid pushing, have her raise her chin and blow or pant lightly whenever she feels her body start to push (the urge to push). This is easier said than done because the urge to push can be so strong. You can pant with her or talk her through it.

Don't expect too much from this technique. It does not take away or diminish her urge to push. All it does is give her a way to keep from adding to the pushing that her body is already doing.

Spontaneous Bearing Down. Once the mother feels like pushing and her cervix is fully dilated or nearly so, her caregiver will give the go-ahead. Then the mother should push spontaneously. Spontaneous bearing down works like this:

1. The contraction begins. The mother focuses her attention as described on page 84.
2. She "greets" the contraction with a big sigh.

3. She simply uses whatever breathing pattern (slow or light) seems best, until her urge to push is so strong that she cannot resist bearing down.

4. The urge to push comes in waves or surges—three to six in each contraction. These surges of the uterus sweep the mother along into an involuntary bearing-down effort (holding her breath or grunting, moaning, or straining) that lasts five to seven seconds.

5. The surge subsides, and she breaths lightly again until the next surge. She continues in this manner until the contraction is over.

6. The contraction ends and she "sighs it away" with her "good-bye" breath.

Directed Pushing. Until 1980 or so, directed pushing was the only bearing-down technique used in virtually every hospital and by virtually all caregivers. Today it is used under the following circumstances:

• When the mother has regional anesthesia and cannot fully feel the urge to push, and so cannot use the spontaneous bearing-down pattern.
• When the baby's descent is too slow with spontaneous bearing down and the caregiver is considering assisting the delivery with instruments—forceps or vacuum extractor (see pages 141–143).
• When directed pushing remains the routine in the institution. Ask her caregiver in advance if the staff advocates spontaneous bearing down or directed pushing.

The directed-pushing technique works like this:

1. The contraction begins. The mother focuses.
2. She "greets" the contraction with her big sigh.
3. She breathes in and out twice; she takes a third breath in and holds it. She holds her breath and strains (pushes) for a fast count of ten, then releases her breath. She takes another quick breath in and repeats the breath holding and straining. She continues in this way until the contraction subsides.
4. The contraction ends. She "sighs it away" with her "good-bye" breath.

Taking Care of Yourself

We sometimes forget that labor can be long and tiring, stressful, and demanding for the birth partner, just as it is for the mother. Losing a night's sleep is never easy. Standing for long periods, skipping meals,

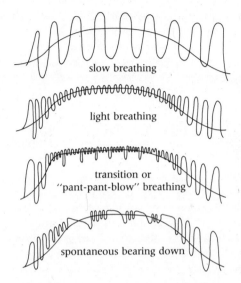

slow breathing

light breathing

transition or "pant-pant-blow" breathing

spontaneous bearing down

Slow breathing consists of long, slow, relaxing breaths. In light breathing, the mother's breaths become lighter and faster as the contraction intensifies. These two patterns are combined in transition, or "pant-pant-blow," breathing. During the birthing stage the mother breathes lightly until she has an urge to push; then she holds her breath or strains.

and offering the mother constant optimism and encouragement are tiring, especially if you are worried or overextended. To be an effective birth partner you will need to pace yourself, draw on the experience and wisdom of others, and look after your own basic needs. This does not necessarily mean taking long breaks for naps or meals, because the mother may not want you to leave. She will probably depend heavily on you to help her through every contraction. There are ways you can take care of her and of yourself at the same time. Here are some suggestions to help you conserve energy and get appropriate help from others:

- Be sure to have your supplies handy. See the list of suggested items for the birth partner's use during labor (page 11).
- Eat and drink tasty, nourishing food and beverages regularly during labor.
- Wear comfortable clothes.
- Rest, by making yourself comfortable near the mother. Don't stand when you can sit. If the mother is lying down and you also need some rest, you can lie down next to her, or sit and rest your head on the bed beside her. If there is enough time between contractions, doze. You will not have trouble waking up to help her if you keep a hand on her arm or belly.
- Ask for reassurance. If you are worried about the length of labor or about the mother's pain or discouragement or fatigue, ask the

caregiver or nurse if everything is all right; express your concerns. It is best, however, to do this outside the mother's hearing.

- Ask the nurse or caregiver for help. If you need ideas for comfort measures, or if you are uncertain whether you are helping the mother enough, ask for suggestions.
- Seek help from another birth partner. Many women have more than one; for example, a relative or friend might be there, along with the husband or lover. The two partners can spell each other at times and work together at others. Some women or couples request the services of a childbirth educator or professional labor support person, who has perspective and experience. A labor support person can raise your morale and the mother's, make concrete suggestions for comfort measures, help you remember some of the things you learned in childbirth class, and remind you and the mother of her Birth Plan. With the unfamiliarity and stress of labor, you might welcome an experienced, calm advocate who can remain with you through the birth.

If you use the above suggestions, not only will you be a more effective birth partner, but you will make your role easier and more personally rewarding.

5

Strategies for Special Situations

Labor, even when perfectly normal, rarely follows a predictable "textbook" pattern. Variations within a range of normal are to be expected. The emotional reactions of women in labor vary, depending on the type of labor pattern they experience. For example, if prelabor or early labor drags on for a long time, the mother may be overcome with exhaustion, worry, or loss of confidence. If, instead, labor starts suddenly with long, painful contractions that threaten to overwhelm the mother, her pain and panic are your main concerns. Women and their birth partners work best with labor when they are open and flexible, and when they are confident that they can and will (with the help of their caregivers) handle whatever comes their way.

This chapter covers situations that require special strategies and special understanding. These situations add stress and require more of the two of you—more resourcefulness, more effort, more reliance on the caregiver, more patience, and more active coaching. The special situations covered here are—

> The Take-Charge Routine (for Labor's Toughest Moments)
> On-the-Spot Coaching (When You Have Had No Preparation Classes)

The Slow-to-Start Labor
The Very Rapid Labor
The Emergency Delivery
When Labor Must Start (Labor-Stimulating Measures)
Backache in Labor
If the Mother Must Labor in Bed
If the Baby Is Breech
The Woman Who Has Had a Previous Disappointing Birth Experience
Incompatibility with the Nurse or Caregiver

The Take-Charge Routine

Reserve this routine for any time during labor when the mother reacts in any of these ways:

- She hits an emotional low.
- She is in despair, weeps, or cries out.
- She wants to give up or feels she cannot go on.
- She is very tense and cannot relax.
- She is in a great deal of pain.

The Take-Charge Routine is exactly that. You move in close and do all you can to help the mother until she regains her inner strength. Usually her despair is brief; with your help she can pass through it and her spirits will rise. Use whatever parts of this routine seem appropriate:

- *Remain calm.* Your touch should be firm and confident. Your voice should remain calm and encouraging.
- *Stay close.* Stay right by her side, your face near hers.
- *Anchor her.* Hold her shoulders or her head in your hands—gently, confidently, firmly—or hold her tightly in your arms.
- *Make eye contact.* Tell her to open her eyes and look at you. Say it loudly enough for her to hear you—but calmly and kindly.
- *Change the ritual she has been using during contractions.* Suggest a different position. Try changing the breathing pattern. Breathe with her or pace her with your hand or voice.
- *Encourage her every breath.* Say "Breathe with me, . . . BREATHE WITH ME. . . . That's the way . . . just like that. . . . Good. . . . STAY WITH IT . . . just like that. . . . LOOK AT ME. . . . Stay with me. . . . Good for you. . . . It's going away. . . . Good. . . . Good. . . . Now just rest, that was so good." You can whisper these words or say

them in a calm, encouraging tone of voice. Sometimes you have to raise your voice to get her attention. But try to keep your tone calm and confident.

- *Talk to her between contractions.* Ask her if what you are doing is helping. Make suggestions: for example, "With the next one, let me help you more. I want you to look at me the moment it starts. We will breathe together so it won't get ahead of us. Okay? Good. You're doing so well. We're really moving now."
- *Repeat yourself.* She may not be able to continue doing what you tell her for more than a few seconds, but that's fine. Say the same things again and help her continue.

What if she says she can't or won't go on? Here are some guidelines:

- *Don't give up on her.* This is a difficult time for her. You cannot help her if you decide she cannot handle it. Acknowledge to her and to yourself that it is difficult, but remind yourselves that it is not impossible.
- *Ask for help and reassurance.* The nurse, caregiver, or another support person can help a lot—measuring dilation, giving you advice, doing some of the coaching, trying something new, even reassuring you that the mother is okay and that this is normal.
- *Remind the mother of her baby.* It may seem surprising, but women can get so caught up in labor that they do not think much about their baby. It may help her to remember why she is going through all this.

What about pain medications? Do you call for them or not? It depends on—

- The mother's prior wishes: Did she want an unmedicated birth? How strongly did she feel about it? (See the "Pain Medications Preference Scale," page 163.) Sometimes asking for pain medications is a way of saying "I need more help."
- Her rate of progress and how far she still has to go.
- How well she responds to your more active coaching.
- Whether she is asking for medications herself and how easily she can be talked out of them.

These considerations can help you decide what to do. It is sometimes difficult to balance present wishes against prior wishes. Try to stick with what the mother wanted before labor regarding the use of medication. But if she insists on changing the plan, respect her wishes.

Numerous women have said, "I never could have done it without my partner. If it hadn't been for him [or her], I would have given up." By using the "Take-Charge Routine," you can indeed get the mother through those desperate moments when she feels she cannot go on; you can truly ease her burden by helping her with every breath.

On-the-Spot Coaching
(When You Have Had No
Childbirth Preparation Classes)

What if labor starts early? What if you and the mother have not taken childbirth classes and have had no time to work together to master the pain-relief techniques described in this book (in chapter 4)? Here are some suggestions: (1) Don't try to learn everything at once while the mother is in labor; (2) use some simple breathing patterns and a few on-the-spot comfort measures; (3) be sure to tell the staff that you and the mother have had no classes. Ask them to show you what to do.

Simple Breathing Patterns

Once the contractions become uncomfortable, the mother can use patterned breathing during each one. You can breathe the pattern with her, verbally coach her through it, or conduct her breathing, setting a pace with rhythmic hand signals. Learn only the *slow breathing pattern* (page 86) to use in early labor and the following simple version of the *light pattern* to use later if she needs it.

Use the light pattern as follows:

1. The contraction begins. Have the mother focus her attention on you or on your voice.
2. The mother takes a big, relaxing sigh.
3. She breathes lightly in and out through her mouth at a rate of about 30 to 120 breaths per minute. She keeps the in-breath silent, but emphasizes the out-breath slightly with an audible blowing sound. You might "conduct" her breathing with rhythmic hand signals to help her pace herself.
4. The contraction ends. The mother takes another big sigh.

On-the-Spot Comfort Measures

In addition to patterned breathing, use the following on-the-spot comfort measures:

Movement and position changes (page 76)
Counterpressure (page 76)
Bath or shower (page 76)
Heat or cold (page 78)
Touch or massage (page 81)
Relaxation (page 83)
Attention-focusing (page 84)
Take-Charge Routine (page 94)

Most of these measures can be used successfully without much preparation. In fact, you can read about them while the mother is in labor and apply them immediately.

The Slow-to-Start Labor

Sometimes it takes hours or days of contractions before the cervix finally lets go and begins to dilate. We don't know exactly why this happens to some women and not to others, but the following conditions seem to predispose a woman to a slow-to-start labor:

• The mother's cervix is thick, firm, and posterior when contractions begin.
• Her cervix is scarred from previous surgery or injury.
• Her uterus is contracting in an uncoordinated fashion, so that the contractions do not open the cervix.
• The baby is high in the mother's pelvis. This is a potential problem for first-time mothers only. In fact, if a woman has had a child before, the baby usually does not drop into the pelvis until after labor is well underway.

Other, unknown, conditions may play a role.

No one can predict the course of the mother's labor, even if some of these conditions exist. Most slow-to-start labors eventually hit their stride and proceed normally after the initial long prelabor period. Some slow-to-start labors, however, are part of a generally prolonged labor, in which all phases proceed, but at a very slow pace. This type of labor presents a serious challenge to the mother and to her birth partner. You cannot know in advance just when her labor will speed up—only time will tell. Your role as birth partner will be to maintain the mother's morale and help her pace herself mentally and physically to accept slow progress.

Strategies for a Slow-to-Start Labor

If the mother's long prelabor is tiring and discouraging, though not necessarily painful, the following measures will help:

- Do not become discouraged yourself. Be patient and confident. This labor will *not* go on forever, and your positive attitude will help the mother keep her spirits up.
- If she is worried, remind her that *a long prelabor does not mean that anything is wrong* with her or the baby. Her cervix simply needs more time before it begins opening. The two of you need to find ways to wait without worrying.
- Call her friends, family, caregiver, or childbirth educator for encouragement and morale boosting.
- Try not to become preoccupied with the labor or to overreact to every contraction. This only makes it seem longer.
- Encourage the mother to eat and drink high-carbohydrate, easily digested foods (for example, toast with jam, cereals, pancakes, pasta, fruit juice, tea with sugar or honey, sorbet or gelatin desserts).

Additionally, you can help her pass the time by rotating among distracting, restful, and labor-stimulating activities. Here are some suggestions:

1. Try *distracting activities* during the day. Encourage the mother to get out of the house. If she is willing, she can visit friends; go for a walk; go to work (let her decide whether she can); go to a movie, the shopping mall, or a restaurant (you can hope you'll have to leave before you're done!). You'll find that when she is out of the house she will try to minimize the contractions. This is easier for her to do when she is among other people than when she's alone at home.

At home you can try these distracting activities: watch TV (programs that *she* likes); dance; play some favorite music; clean, straighten up, pay bills; play games; start a time-consuming project, like baking bread or painting a crib (she will almost hope that labor doesn't start until the project is finished!); fix meals for after the baby is born; have friends over, especially to relieve you if you are tired.

2. Help her *rest or sleep* at night, or nap during the day, if possible. If she is tired and cannot sleep, try the following:

- Suggest a bath. Fill the tub with warm (not hot) water; attach an inflatable bathtub pillow or folded towels for a headrest. She should plan to stay in the tub for a long time; you may have to add hot water from time to time. Rest and sleep come more easily in a warm bath. Keep an eye on her; make sure she doesn't slip down so her head goes under the water.

- Encourage her to try a long shower. You might need to turn up the water heater.
- Give her a soothing massage.
- Give her a relaxing beverage (warm milk, herbal tea).

3. Try *labor-stimulating measures* for periods of one or two hours at a time to initiate stronger, more frequent contractions. Follow the guidelines in "When Labor Must Start," page 105, noting the precautions for these procedures.

If the mother is in pain, long baths, relaxation, massage, and slow patterned breathing will help. See "Comfort Measures," page 73, for ideas.

If *you* are worried that the mother won't have the stamina to cope with "real" labor after this prolonged prelabor, remind yourself—and her—that she is well equipped at this time in her life to cope with a long period without sleep. Women's energy levels increase before labor as their bodies gear up for the physical demands ahead. The mother may handle it better than you do! The nesting urge is evidence of this extraordinary bodily adjustment. Try to have confidence that, although it may be difficult, the odds are excellent that she will have the energy it takes to handle the later phases of labor.

The Very Rapid Labor

Some women have labors that start with hard, frequent, painful contractions and are over in a matter of a few hours. It seems the mother barely has time to adjust to being in labor before the baby is born. Or, sometimes only the first (dilation) stage is rapid: the cervix dilates so quickly that the mother can't catch up mentally; but then, in the second (birthing) stage, the uterus takes a long rest. If that happens, the mother has to cope with the difficulties of both fast and slow labors. It is impossible to predict which women will labor in these ways, but a rapid labor seems to be more likely if—

- The mother has had a rapid or quicker-than-average (less than ten hours) labor before. A second or third labor tends to be faster than the first.
- Her cervix is very soft, thin, and already partially dilated before labor begins; and if the baby is low in the mother's pelvis in a favorable position.

Few women or their birth partners are prepared for a rapid labor, especially after reading and learning about typical labor patterns and prolonged prelabors. If the mother's labor starts rapidly, she will be caught off guard: she was expecting the early contractions to be gentle, short, and far apart; but her labor begins instead with contractions that are long, painful, and close together—like the contractions of the transition phase.

How Is the Mother Likely to React?

You can expect the following reactions from the mother if her labor begins rapidly:

- *Shock and disbelief.* She may not be able to respond constructively. She may not realize that this is real labor.
- *Fear or panic.* She may think that something is terribly wrong—that she or the baby is in danger. Or, she may be frightened that she cannot reach you, her caregiver, or anyone for help; or that she cannot get to the hospital in time.
- *Loss of confidence.* If the mother thinks these are the "easy" contractions of early labor, she may lose all confidence that she can cope with labor once it progresses.
- *Dependence on you.* She may barely be able to change positions between contractions, let alone get ready to go to the hospital. She may need your constant help to cope with the contractions.

How Should You React?

- Believe what you see. If the mother is shaky, in pain, having strong, fast contractions, don't assume she is overreacting to early labor. Assume she is having a hard labor and move right into a leadership role in helping her cope.
- Use the "Take-Charge Routine" (page 94) if she has trouble with the contractions.
- Don't lose faith in her. Don't decide she has less fortitude than you thought. Her response truly reflects how hard this labor is.
- Call the caregiver, go to the hospital, or both. Drive carefully, but don't waste time.

The Emergency Delivery

What if it is too late to get to the hospital? What if you and the mother are on your own—in your car or at home? How will you know if it's too late to go to the hospital? What if the baby is coming? If this is a planned home birth, what if the midwife has not arrived? You will know that it is too late to go to the hospital if (1) the mother says she can feel the baby coming out; (2) you can see the baby's head at her vaginal opening; or (3) she is pushing forcibly and cannot stop.

If all of this happens at home, stay there and call 911 or the operator for an emergency vehicle with a paramedical team.

If all this happens in the car, pull over to the side of the road, put on your flasher lights, and tend to the mother's needs. If the weather is cold, leave the motor running and the heater on—you don't want the baby to get chilled once he is born. (Be sure the emergency brake is on!)

Basic Rules for an Emergency Delivery

Before the birth, this is what you do:

- Believe the mother if she says the baby is coming.
- Remain calm (at least try to act calm!).
- Get help—from paramedics, friends or neighbors, even children.
- Turn up the heat in the car or at home.
- Gather blankets, towels, or warm clothing to wrap the baby in.
- Find newspapers, a bowl, paper towels, or a plastic bag to hold the placenta.
- Reassure the mother. Point out that when labor happens this fast, it's because there's *nothing* holding it up; in fact, everything is working *too* well.
- Help the mother breathe through her contractions. She SHOULD NOT PUSH. Help her pant or blow lightly with her chin up when her body starts to push. This is to slow the delivery.
- Help the mother lie down on her side or recline in a semisitting position if possible; this is preferable to squatting or standing. Lying down may slow the delivery slightly, and it ensures that the baby will have a safe place to land as he comes out.
- Get ready to catch the baby. Have something ready to dry and cover the baby immediately (towels, blanket, your shirt or jacket).
- Make sure the baby lands in a soft place (on the bed or the seat of the car), and does not drop. Babies come out fast and are very wet and slippery, so you may not be able to catch him. If the woman is standing or squatting, or if there is no soft place for the baby to land, place your body so that the baby will land on you if you don't catch him.
- Wash your hands thoroughly, if possible, but this is not so important that you should leave the mother if she needs you badly or if the baby is coming out.

As the baby comes out, this is what you do:

- Help the mother to pant, not push.
- Wipe the baby's face and head when it emerges. If the membranes of the bag of waters cover the baby's face (which is very unlikely), tear them with your fingernail or remove them by pulling at them with a towel so the baby can breathe. When the baby's head is out, it will turn toward one side, and then the shoulders and body will probably be born with the next contraction.
- Catch the baby.
- Wipe the baby off and quickly place him naked on his side or stomach on his mother's naked abdomen. Cover him (including his head but not his face) with a blanket, towel, or clothing. It is critical to keep the baby dry and warm. You'll want to be able to see his face to monitor his condition.
- Check the baby's breathing. Babies normally begin breathing or crying within seconds after birth. Wipe away any mucus, blood, or vernix (a white, creamy substance that may be found all over the baby) from his nostrils or mouth.
- Rub the baby's head, back, or chest briskly or slap the soles of his feet if he doesn't begin breathing right away. He might sputter and choke out some mucus or fluid from his airway.
- Don't lay the baby on his back; that position would make it harder for him to get rid of any fluids that might be in his nose, mouth, or chest. Place the baby on his side or, preferably, on his stomach with his head lower than his body. This "safety position" is the best to promote breathing. Be sure the baby's face is clear for breathing and not pressed into the mother's body.

The Cord and the Placenta. Don't worry about the cord at all. You do not need to cut it or tie it. Changes within the cord cause compression of the blood vessels and stop blood flow through the cord within a few minutes after the birth.

The placenta will probably be born within fifteen to thirty minutes after the baby is born. If it seems slow in coming, have the mother stand or squat. Do not pull on the cord—just let it come. Catch the placenta in a bowl, a towel, a blanket, or in a piece of clothing. Place it near the baby's body. It will be bloody and messy, but it is otherwise not a problem.

Care of the Mother. You can expect some bleeding from the mother's vagina, but if it looks like more than two cups of blood, she may be losing too much. Do the following, whether the mother is bleeding excessively or not:

- Place the baby at the mother's breast as soon as possible after delivery (when you know he is breathing and even before the placenta comes, if the cord is long enough to allow it). The baby's suckling or just nuzzling at the breast helps contract the uterus and slow down any bleeding.
- Feel the mother's abdomen for her uterus by pressing into the area below her navel. It should feel hard and firm, like a large grapefruit. If you cannot feel the uterus, it is because it is too relaxed. You should get it to contract tightly because *a relaxed uterus bleeds too much*. (See "When the Mother Bleeds Excessively," below.)

Once both mother and baby appear to be all right, you should get them to the hospital for a thorough checkup. The mother might need stitches; the baby will need to have his cord cared for and to have a physical exam. Other procedures may be appropriate as well.

Your caregiver (especially if you had originally planned a home birth) or the paramedical team will probably have arrived by this time. You will be very relieved. Some day, this will make a great story to tell at parties and baby showers!

First Aid for Emergencies in Childbirth

What if the birth doesn't go so normally? You should know a little about this possibility, just in case a complication arises.

The two major complications of emergency deliveries are these: the mother bleeds excessively or the baby does not begin to breathe. These complications, though rare, can present real dangers. The following discussion explains what to do if they happen. Of course, if you have had time to call an ambulance, you will very likely have medical help soon; but you must know what to do until help arrives.

When the Mother Bleeds Excessively. The mother will have some bleeding, but if it looks as if she is losing more than two cups of blood, or if she gets weak and pale and her skin feels clammy, she may be losing too much. This could happen because of bleeding from the uterus, before or after the placenta comes out, or because of bleeding from open wounds in the vagina or perineum (the area between the vagina and the anus) caused by the rapid birth. Following are some guidelines for preventing excessive bleeding.

If the placenta is out, get the uterus to contract in these ways:

1. *Stimulate the mother's nipples.* Having the baby suckle at the breast is most effective; try this first. If the baby is not ready to suckle, try rolling the nipples between your fingers (or have the mother do it herself). Roll both nipples at the same time or roll one while the baby suckles at the other.

2. *Massage the top of the uterus* (the fundus) in her lower abdomen with one or both hands vigorously until the uterus contracts. This is painful to the mother, but do not stop until the uterus hardens. It will feel like a grapefruit, in size and consistency, when it has contracted.

If the placenta has not come out within thirty minutes, try stimulating the mother's nipples and help her to squat or stand. You must get her to the hospital to have the placenta removed if these measures are not immediately successful. *Do not pull on the cord.*

It is very hard to tell if the source of excessive bleeding is a tear or laceration (cut) in the vagina or perineum. But if you can see that there is a tear or laceration, place ice wrapped in a wet cloth or towel in the vagina and apply firm pressure. Go to the hospital.

When the Baby Does Not Begin to Breathe. If the baby does not begin to breathe within two minutes after you have wiped fluids away from her nose and mouth, you need to use infant CPR (cardiopulmonary resuscitation):

1. Rub the baby briskly.
2. Check the baby's mouth and remove any blobs of mucus you find.
3. Lay the baby on her back, and gently bend her head back.
4. Place your mouth over both the baby's nose and mouth, and, with your hand on her chest, blow gently until her chest rises a little. Repeat this every three seconds until the baby breathes on her own or until help arrives. *Don't blow hard:* a baby's lungs are tiny. You need to blow only enough to make the baby's chest rise.
5. Get to the hospital as soon as possible.

When the midwife or paramedical team arrives or you get to the hospital, the emergency personnel will have drugs to contract the uterus, intravenous fluids, oxygen and resuscitation equipment to help the baby breathe, and (in the hospital) everything they need to remove a retained placenta. Most hospitals are ready for immediate action.

You will probably feel lost in the shuffle. Try to stay with the mother or the baby, but recognize that in an obstetric emergency, immediate action is the primary concern and you must not impede it in any way. In a true emergency, there may be no time until afterwards for explanations or answers to your questions.

When Labor Must Start (Labor-Stimulating Measures)

Under some circumstances, the caregiver decides that delaying or awaiting the baby's birth for much longer carries unacceptable risks to mother or baby. Then, the caregiver must consider artificially inducing labor (starting labor with drugs or by breaking the bag of waters). The caregiver will consider inducing labor under the following circumstances:

- The mother has an illness such as diabetes, heart disease, lung disease, or high blood pressure.
- There is no herpes lesion in a woman who has been plagued by frequent outbreaks of herpes, and her due date is near.
- The pregnancy has lasted more than forty-two weeks.
- The bag of waters has been broken for a prolonged period.
- The fetus has grown slowly and is small (because of poor functioning of the placenta).
- The fetus seems overly stressed in the uterus.

Under other circumstances, such as a prolonged prelabor or a slow-down in active labor, the caregiver, the mother, or both may want to speed up or strengthen (augment) the contractions.

The mother may be able to start labor herself by using the following measures. If she is successful, she can avoid a medical induction of labor, which tends to be risky and invasive. (See "Induction and Augmentation of Labor," page 135.) If she is not successful, she may become discouraged, and she may end up with an induction anyway.

Before using these techniques to stimulate labor, be sure the mother discusses them with her caregiver. She should ask the caregiver for advice about whether to stimulate contractions and how to do it.

Nipple Stimulation

Stimulating the mother's nipples causes the release of oxytocin, a hormone that contracts the uterus. Taking advantage of this physiological connection between breast and uterus brings a high degree of success, either in starting labor or in softening the cervix. It will not work, however, in a woman who is currently breastfeeding a toddler. Her body has adapted to the increased levels of oxytocin already present due to the continuing nipple stimulation.

Methods of Nipple Stimulation. The following measures might need to be repeated after a few hours or after half a day. Either you or the mother can stimulate the nipples in the following ways:

- Lightly stroke, roll, or brush one or both nipples with the fingertips. Often, within a few minutes the mother will have stronger contractions. You or she may need to continue this stimulation for hours to keep the contractions coming.
- Massage the breasts gently with warm, moist towels for an hour at a time, three times a day.
- Caress, lick, or suck the mother's nipples, or roll them between your fingers. Try this for as long as the mother finds it effective and pleasant, or until her contractions become strong.
- Use a gentle, but powerful, institutional-quality electric breast pump (available in hospitals). A nurse can show her what to do. Manual or battery-operated breast pumps are less likely to be useful.
- Nurse a borrowed baby. Suckling a three- to twelve-week-old baby seems to be the most effective form of nipple stimulation. At this age babies are usually efficient nursers but are not too fussy to suckle at the breast of someone besides their mother. The woman's midwife or childbirth educator may be able to help her find the right baby.

   The baby needs to be awake and not very hungry. A sleepy baby will not suck, and a hungry baby gets frustrated by the lack of milk. The baby's fussy period is a good time, because the baby often wants simply to suck and will effectively stimulate the nipples.

   Before nursing a borrowed baby, the mother should wash her breasts and hands. Because her waters may break, she should sit on a waterproof pad. She should try to suckle the baby for at least ten minutes on each side.

   If the mother is ill, she should not try this—the baby could catch her illness.

If the mother is uncomfortable with the idea of nursing someone else's baby, try other methods of stimulating labor (beginning on page 107).

Precautions When Using Nipple Stimulation. While many caregivers are very comfortable with this method of bringing on contractions, others are wary of nipple stimulation because it may cause excessively long or strong contractions. These caregivers worry that strong contractions may stress the fetus, especially if the mother is at high risk for complications. Before advising nipple stimulation, the caregiver may want to check the fetal response to such stimulation by performing a contraction stress test (page 130). Also, take the following precautions to help avoid excessively strong or long contractions:

1. Time the length and assess the intensity of all contractions resulting from nipple stimulation.
2. Begin with "low-dose," intermittent stimulation and work up as needed. At first, stimulate one nipple until the mother has a contraction; then stop until the contraction is over. Repeat. Try this for four to six contractions.
3. If stimulating only one nipple does not cause any contractions in a reasonable length of time, or if the contractions the mother is already having do not increase in frequency, length, or strength, try stimulating both breasts intermittently, then, if necessary, both breasts continuously. Having the mother nurse a baby is probably the most effective form of stimulation.
4. Stop altogether if the "low-dose" stimulation results in contractions that are painful or long (over sixty seconds).

Walking

Although it is more effective in speeding a slow labor, walking may also help to get labor started. You might try a fairly brisk walk, but don't go too far away from home or the labor room.

Acupressure

Certain acupressure (*shiatsu*) points can be activated to stimulate contractions. Although acupressure is little understood in Western cultures, it is widely practiced in the Far East for health purposes. One point, Spleen 6, is considered a powerful point; when pressure is applied there, it can induce contractions of the uterus. Wataru Ohashi and Mary Hoover, in their book, *Natural Childbirth, The Eastern Way* (see "Recommended Resources"), caution that this point should not be pressed before the mother's due date.

Use acupressure in the following way to stimulate contractions:

1. Locate Spleen 6, about four finger breadths above the inner ankle on the shinbone. This is a very tender spot.
2. Press the Spleen 6 point hard with the tip of your thumb. Press at an angle from behind the mother's leg, in and toward the front of

her leg. See the illustration and further discussion of Spleen 6 on page 82.

3. Apply the pressure three times for ten to fifteen seconds at a time, resting a few seconds in between.

4. Repeat the cycle every few minutes if the pressure seems to be causing contractions.

Sexual Stimulation

Sexual excitement, particularly orgasm, causes release of oxytocin and contractions of the uterus. Sexual excitement may also cause the release of other hormonelike substances (prostaglandins), which soften the cervix. Prostaglandins are also present in semen. Clitoral stimulation, even without orgasm or intercourse, may also be effective.

If you choose these methods of stimulation, make them as pleasant as possible. Try to forget your goal of starting labor and free yourselves to enjoy the sexual experience.

There are a few precautions to follow when using these methods:

1. You may use intercourse, manual stimulation of the clitoris, and oral sexual stimulation as long as the mother's bag of waters is intact, but avoid placing anything within the vagina if the membranes have ruptured, because doing so would increase the risk of infection.

2. Never blow into the vagina during pregancy.

3. Modify or avoid these methods if either of you has any sores that could spread or if the mother has an uncomfortable vaginal condition.

Bowel Stimulation

By stimulating and emptying her bowels, the mother may be able to start labor. Some experts believe this method stimulates labor by increasing the mother's level of prostaglandins, which are produced when the bowel contracts. The prostaglandins cause the cervix to soften and thin. The mother can use an enema or castor oil to stimulate the bowels.

Enemas. An enema may start labor by causing enough bowel action to activate contractions of the uterus. You can buy a complete, compact, disposable enema unit, with instructions included, at a drugstore. At home, the mother can give the enema to herself, or you can help her with it. The mother might also be able to get an enema at the hospital.

Castor Oil. A laxative, castor oil may cause powerful contractions of the bowel. It has been used to induce labor for years and years, with some success. Follow these guidelines:

1. Give the mother two to four tablespoons of unflavored castor oil at first. It is more palatable if you mix it with an equal amount of orange juice and a teaspoon of baking soda; stir it fast. She should drink it quickly.

2. One-half hour later, the mother may take another two tablespoons in the same way, and after another half-hour, another two tablespoons.

3. The mother should stop taking the castor oil after a maximum of three doses.

Castor oil causes cramping and diarrhea, and when it works contractions pick up within hours or half a day. Do not expect contractions immediately.

Teas and Tinctures

Some midwives and physicians use certain herbal teas or tinctures (for example, blue or black cohosh tea) to bring on or speed up contractions. Use these teas or tinctures only under the guidance of her caregiver, as dosage and strength should be individualized.

Backache in Labor

One woman in four feels intense backache during labor contractions. This is what you need to know about so-called back labor:

- Back labor is usually the result of the baby's position—head down, facing forward in the mother's body, with the back of the head pressing against the mother's low spine. This is called the OP (occiput posterior) position and it causes intense pain in the low spine. (See "Position," page 36.)
- Relaxation and breathing are usually not enough to cope with the pain of back labor.
- Most OP babies rotate spontaneously during labor, turning their heads until the back of the head is pointing toward the mother's front (in the OA, or occiput anterior, position). This rotation can take place at any time during labor—early or late. There is often a delay in dilation in the active phase while the baby's head rotates.
- Once the baby has rotated, the back pain usually subsides, and labor resumes progress.

- Occasionally, the baby does not rotate by itself, with the following possible consequences: (1) labor may be very slow if the baby is also large; (2) the baby may be born facing forward ("sunny-side-up"), though such a birth is rare; (3) the caregiver may assist rotation with forceps after the cervix is fully dilated; (4) a cesarean delivery may be the solution if vaginal birth appears too difficult.
- You *can* help the mother deal with backache in labor by (1) encouraging the baby to rotate and (2) using specific comfort measures to relieve the mother's back pain.

Encourage the Baby to Rotate

Find out the position of the baby. The mother may be able to figure out its position by locating the places she feels most of the baby's small movements, like kicking and punching: the baby's hand and foot movements are probably directly opposite where its back is. The nurse or caregiver can also usually tell where it is by palpating the mother's abdomen and feeling parts of the baby. If the back of the baby's head is pressing against the mother's back, the mother will feel most of the baby's small movements in the front of her abdomen, on the left or right side or in the center.

Once you know that the baby is in an OP position, help the mother to use different body positions, pelvic rocking, and abdominal stroking to encourage the baby to turn. Even if you are not sure that the baby is OP, if the mother has backache during her contractions, try these measures. They tend to relieve discomfort, and they will *not* turn an OA baby into an OP position.

Positions and Movement for Back Labor. The mother should use one position for twenty to thirty minutes at a time, then try another. See the illustrations (page 79) of positions for labor.

- *Hands and knees.* The mother should spend time on her hands and knees, or resting on her knees and leaning forward with her upper body on a chair, a bed, or your lap (some labor beds can be arranged to support the mother in this position). This will allow gravity to help the baby turn.
- *Pelvic rocking.* While on her hands and knees, the mother rocks her pelvis forward and back (alternately arching her back by tucking her pelvis under, and straightening her back, returning her pelvis to its normal position) or she swivels her pelvis in a circle. This helps free the baby within the pelvis, encouraging it to rotate.
- *Standing and walking.* Some experts believe the alignment of the

baby with the pelvis is most favorable when the mother is standing. In addition, walking allows some movement within the pelvic joints, which may encourage the baby to rotate. Further, many women find standing and walking much more comfortable than lying down or sitting.

Abdominal Stroking. If you know where the baby's back is (your caregiver may be able to tell you), begin a firm stroke there, and stroke toward where you want the baby's back to go. You will be stroking from the far side of the mother's abdomen (left or right) toward the center of her abdomen. It's almost as if you are gently pressing the baby around. This should feel very good to the mother. If you cannot do it so that it feels good, stop, and focus on the other measures to turn the baby.

Comfort Measures for Backache

Along with the measures already suggested for turning the baby, there are some comfort measures that are particularly useful in reducing back pain. These comfort measures are described in chapter 4, and they include the following:

> Counterpressure (page 76)
> Massage (page 81)
> Heat and cold (page 78)
> Baths and showers (page 76)
> Transcutaneous electrical nerve stimulation (TENS) (page 80)

If the Mother Must Labor in Bed

Sometimes a woman must remain in bed for labor and birth. These are the most common reasons:

- The mother has high blood pressure. A woman's blood pressure tends to lower when she lies on her left side.
- The mother's membranes have ruptured (the bag of waters has broken). Some caregivers believe that the danger of prolapsed cord (see page 153) increases if a woman stands up after her bag of waters breaks. These caregivers require the mother to lie down throughout labor. (Other caregivers assess the situation individually because they believe that the upright position sometimes *protects against* prolapsed cord.)

- The mother has used pain medications. If a woman is sleepy or groggy, or if part of her body is numb, she is safest staying in bed.
- The mother needs to use equipment that attaches her to machines. Intravenous fluids, electric infusion pumps (for pitocin drip), electronic fetal monitors, catheters, and others all tend to make it difficult or impossible for the woman to move out of bed.
- It is the hospital's custom. In many hospitals women are routinely discouraged from leaving their beds. There is no medical reason for such a practice.

Being restricted to bed may present no particular problems for the mother, especially if it does not add to her pain, or if she had not expected to do anything else. Many women, however, find lying down to be most uncomfortable. Some women become very restless and are unable to stay down. If they had planned to use movement and positioning for comfort or to help their labors progress, they will be disappointed and may try to change their caregiver's orders.

Sometimes restricting a woman to bed slows her labor and increases the pain from contractions. She is also prevented from doing many of the things that speed labor and increase her comfort.

Here are some things you should do:

1. Find out why she is confined to bed. You may be able to persuade the caregiver to change the orders if there is no compelling medical reason for the mother to remain in bed. If bed rest is medically necessary, you will both be better able to accept it and cooperate if you understand why.

2. Find out how strict the order is. The mother may be told not to leave the bed, or she may be told not to turn from her left side at all. She may be allowed up for short periods or to go to the bathroom. She may be able to change positions in bed or to stand or sit near the bed.

3. Help her focus on the many pain-coping techniques and comfort measures she can use while in bed, without dwelling too much on what she cannot do. Try relaxation (page 83); patterned breathing (page 85); attention-focusing (page 84); spontaneous rituals (page 74); counterpressure, massage, and acupressure (pages 76, 81, and 82); heat and cold (page 78); Transcutaneous Electrical Nerve Stimulation (TENS) (page 80); hypnosis (page 83); or the "Take-Charge Routine" (page 94).

Remaining in bed sometimes adds to the mother's stress, but, with your help, she can probably handle this challenge. The key is to understand and agree with the reasons she must remain in bed, to focus on the techniques she can still use, and to make sure she has excellent labor support.

If The Baby Is Breech

In late pregnancy, about one in thirty babies is in a breech presentation (with their head up and buttocks or feet, or both, down at the mother's cervix). There are three types of breech presentation: the *frank* breech, with the buttocks down at the cervix; the *complete* breech, with the knees bent so that both buttocks and feet are down at the cervix; and the *footling* breech, with one or both feet down at the cervix. The breech presentation causes difficulties during delivery, particularly for premature or very large babies, and for the footling and complete breeches. Briefly, the problems are as follows:

- The cord is more likely to prolapse (see page 153), especially in footling and complete breech presentations.
- Other difficulties are due mostly to the fact that the head is born last. Sometimes there is a delay in the birth of the head, because it is the largest part of the baby. Sometimes the baby inhales amniotic fluid and vaginal secretions, which interfere with breathing after birth. Also, while still inside, the head can pinch the cord while the baby still depends on it for oxygen.

Because of these risks, the following procedures may be recommended during late pregnancy, either to turn the baby to a head-down presentation, or to deliver the baby safely.

Breech Tilt. At between thirty-two and thirty-five weeks' gestation, the mother may begin using the *breech tilt* position to encourage her baby to turn, as follows:

1. Three times a day, when her stomach is not full and her baby is active, she lies on the floor on her back with her knees bent and feet flat. She raises her hips twelve inches or more. You slide cushions beneath her hips to hold her in the tilted position. She is now lying with her head and shoulders on the floor and her hips and knees raised. The same position can be achieved by having her lie on an ironing board with one end propped on a couch.

2. She remains there for ten to fifteen minutes (less if she is uncomfortable).

3. As she consciously releases tension in her abdomen and trunk,

she visualizes her baby's head pressing "down" against the top of the uterus, and the baby trying to get her head "up" again. The position seems to encourage some babies to turn.

Music. If she has high blood pressure or cannot tolerate the breech tilt position, she should avoid it and concentrate on using music for the same purpose. Place stereo earphones low on the mother's abdomen and play rhythmic music moderately loud. Some people believe babies particularly like baroque music. The baby may try to move her head closer so she can hear the music better. The music can be used with or without the breech tilt position. It seems to work sometimes.

Most babies who are breech at thirty-two or thirty-three weeks turn spontaneously before birth; it is not clear whether these techniques improve the chance that a baby will turn. I recommend them since I feel they are harmless, and may be helpful.

Breech Version. If the baby is breech at thirty-seven or thirty-eight weeks' gestation, the mother and her caregiver may want to try an *external version*, a procedure for turning a breech baby. Versions have been done over the years in many cultures. This is how they are done today in a medical setting:

1. The mother goes to the office or hospital. An ultrasound scan is performed to confirm the breech presentation, and to assess the size and heart rate of the fetus, the location of the placenta, the amount of amniotic fluid, and other conditions.

2. The mother may be given an injection of terbutaline, which relaxes the uterus.

3. She lies down on her back and relaxes.

4. The doctor (midwives do not do these versions) rubs a lubricant on the mother's abdomen and, with the guidance of ultrasound, presses on her abdomen to lift the baby out of the pelvis and gradually turn the baby around so the head is down. If unsuccessful at first the doctor may try once or twice more, but that is all.

5. The mother remains as relaxed as possible; your help with this makes a big difference.

6. After the procedure, the mother undergoes a nonstress test (page 130) to see that the baby has tolerated the procedure well.

Although the version procedure has many built-in safeguards, most caregivers notify the labor and delivery floor that they are doing it, so if a serious problem should arise, such as prolapsed cord, fetal distress, or bleeding, a cesarean could be performed at once.

Versions are successful 60 to 70 percent of the time. Most of the women who undergo versions have vaginal births and healthy outcomes for mother and baby.

When a version is not successful a vaginal birth may be planned, if (1) the caregiver is experienced in vaginal breech births; (2) the baby is no larger than average size; (3) the baby is in a frank breech presentation (only the buttocks are down); (4) the baby's chin is down toward the chest; and (5) the mother's pelvis appears to be of adequate size.

If all these conditions are not present, a cesarean birth is planned to assure the best possible outcome. The cesarean rate for breech presentation is very high in North America.

The Woman Who Has Had a Previous Disappointing Birth Experience

Most women who have gone through labor have some doubts about whether they can "do it again." For those whose previous birth experiences were normal and satisfying, confidence and optimism tend to outweigh apprehension or doubt. But, for those who have had disappointing birth experiences, such as a cesarean birth, a difficult or traumatic birth, or a premature, sick, disabled, or stillborn baby, the memories of those past difficulties may keep coming back. As these women approach and anticipate the upcoming labor and birth, they may be haunted by various doubts and anxieties. For example, they may not feel confident about being able to cope with childbirth again; they may be anxious about their safety, especially if their previous labor ended in a cesarean or in a difficult forceps or vacuum delivery; or they may be worried about the baby, especially if they had a baby who did not survive or who was very ill.

If the mother has had a difficult birth before she will benefit from special preparation for labor and special understanding and support during labor. The following suggestions should help you to help her:

• Find a support group or a class that helps women and their birth partners prepare during pregnancy for these special labors (for example, VBAC [vaginal birth after cesarean] classes for women who want to have a vaginal delivery after having had a cesarean; or Pregnancy After Loss groups for couples who have lost a baby and are expecting again). These classes and meetings help the mother realize that she is not the only woman troubled by a previous difficult birth, and that she *can* cope. They also teach the birth partner how to be especially helpful during labor. Ask the caregiver or the hospital for the names of instructors or leaders of these classes and groups.

• Find a good book that discusses birth preparation after a woman has had a cesarean or a difficult or disappointing birth. Find a book that deals with the mother's particular problem. (See "Recommended Resources".)

• Learn about labor and how to be a birth partner by reading this book and by taking childbirth classes, because the mother will need especially sensitive and capable labor support.

• Consider using the services of an experienced labor support person. Many childbirth educators, nurses, and others with training and experience provide professional labor support. They can offer you and the mother their experienced perspective, steady encouragement, and specific help; they can also work with you and the staff as go-betweens or advocates. They may or may not charge a fee for their services.

• Anticipate the mother's unique emotional needs. Besides the typical emotional responses to labor (covered in chapters 2 and 3), there are some additional emotional hurdles that the woman who has had a disappointing past experience may have to overcome during labor. They are described here, along with suggestions about how you can help:

Early labor. As she gets into labor, the mother may suddenly lose heart. This is her "moment of truth," and she may be flooded with self-doubt. She will need your encouragement and understanding. Review "Getting into Labor," page 33, and "The Slow-to-Start Labor," page 97, for ideas about helping the mother get into labor both mentally and physically.

Flashbacks to the previous labor. At times, the mother may not be able to escape the feeling that her labor is "just like last time," especially if events in the present labor trigger unpleasant associations with the previous labor. This is normal; you can help by acknowledging the similarity of the two labors, by discussing the mother's feelings, and, most important, by reminding her that this is not "last time" but a completely new labor that she must deal with as such.

The point in labor at which she had the cesarean or other difficulty before. Some women feel a great deal of apprehension before they reach this critical point, and are relieved only after it has passed. Try to help the mother with distraction and stress-reduction measures (see "Comfort Measures for Labor," page 73), and then rejoice with her when she has passed beyond her critical point.

A great potential for healing and growth exists when a woman confronts her difficult memories and deals constructively with them. With preparation beforehand and sensitive, capable support during labor, the mother's experience of birth is almost certain to be far more satisfying and fulfilling than her previous experience was.

Incompatibility with the Nurse or Caregiver

One disadvantage of the North American system of maternity care is that the mother is usually cared for by people she has never met. She hardly ever knows her nurses; she scarcely knows her doctor, whom she may have met briefly six or eight times during her pregnancy. And if her own doctor is not on call when she goes into labor, she will be assisted by a substitute doctor who may be a complete stranger. The kind of care typically given by midwives is an exception: spending time with the mother and getting to know her is one of the features of midwifery.

Most of the time no serious problems arise, and the mother, her caregiver, and the nurses get along quite well. What do you do, though, if one or both of you is uncomfortable with the nurse or caregiver? Differences in attitudes toward childbirth, in personality, or in perceptions of each other's roles sometimes become obvious during labor. Discomfort or friction may arise. This *never* works in the mother's best interests. She needs to be surrounded by kind people who she believes will encourage and support her. Usually, problems with the staff are not serious and can easily be resolved. The following are some suggestions for avoiding, minimizing, or solving conflicts:

- Do not be the cause of any friction yourself. By your attitude and your behavior show that you are friendly and polite, that you expect to work well with the staff, and that you appreciate their experience and the contributions they can make to the mother's comfort and well-being. If you appear suspicious, frightened, or hostile, the staff might react defensively.
- Make an effort to communicate any special concerns you or the mother have: for example, a desire for natural childbirth, a fear of needles or blood, and so forth.
- Bring a copy of the mother's Birth Plan with you. If there is time, discuss the Birth Plan and ask if the nurse or caregiver will help you to follow the plan as closely as possible. If the staff have any concerns about the Birth Plan, it is better to discuss them than to ignore them. Differences can usually be resolved easily.

- Call the nurse or caregiver by name.
- If there are differences between you or the mother and the nurse, try one or more of the following tactics:

  Deal with the nurse politely. Say, for example, "I cannot talk with you during contractions because I need to help [the mother] breathe and relax"; or "I think there is a misunderstanding. Our doctor said it would be fine for [the mother] to walk around and use the shower. Would you please check with her doctor?"

  Talk to the head nurse. Explain any differences you and the nurse have in a nonaccusatory way and ask the head nurse to assign another nurse or to help mediate the problem.

  Talk directly to the mother's caregiver. If there is an apparent misunderstanding over the nurse's management of labor, ask the caregiver to take care of it.
- If the problem is with the doctor or midwife (especially if this is someone the mother has never met before), you can try to discuss it directly. If this doesn't solve the problem, ask the nurse to intervene on the mother's behalf and to advocate for her. Or, if the problem involves a clinical decision, ask for a second opinion.
- Balance the stress that a confrontation will cause against the amount of emotional or physical discomfort resulting from the current arrangement. Sometimes the best interests of the mother are served by avoiding conflict rather than by resolving it—in other words, you may have to accept a less-than-ideal arrangement and work with it.
- If, before labor, you or the mother *anticipates* problems, *be sure* to prepare and discuss a Birth Plan. And consider hiring an experienced labor support person to work with the two of you ahead of time and during labor—to help smooth relations with the staff and to act as an advocate.
- If you are stuck with a nurse or caregiver with whom you are incompatible and who will not yield, you should accept the situation for the moment and focus your energies on helping the mother cope. You may feel powerless and frustrated under these circumstances, but you cannot stop labor while the problem gets settled. And trying to correct a serious communication problem in the midst of labor might make the labor harder and more stressful for the mother. After the baby is born, you can pursue the matter in an effort to satisfy your frustration and to enlighten those responsible for patient care. While this effort will probably not benefit the mother, baby, or yourself, your efforts may help prevent similar difficulties for another laboring woman in the future.

Part Three

THE MEDICAL SIDE
OF CHILDBIRTH

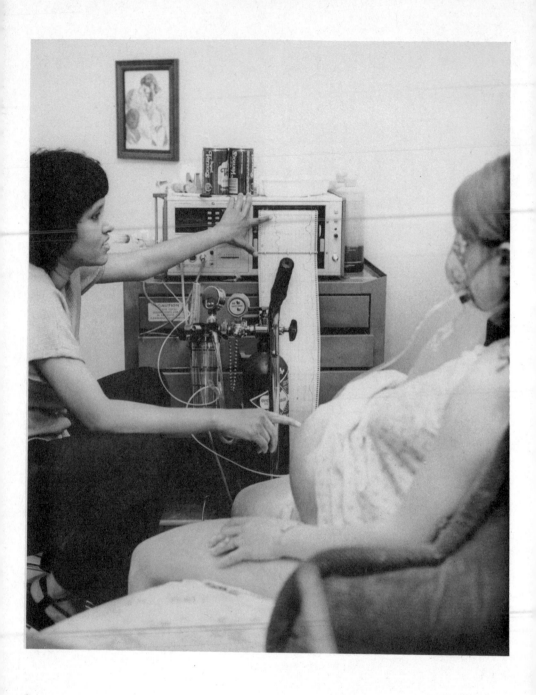

*T*HE CAREGIVER'S PRIMARY ROLE IN CHILDBIRTH IS TO safeguard the health of mother and child. Throughout pregnancy, the caregiver relies on a wide assortment of tests, technologies, and procedures to detect problems before they become serious. Similar tests and technologies are available during childbirth.

Caregivers differ among themselves regarding what should constitute routine basic care during childbirth. Some caregivers use many medical procedures (interventions) in every labor; others use them only when problems are suspected. Pregnant woman differ among themselves over the same issue. Some feel more secure with a highly medical approach, while others are wary of this approach, preferring to place more trust in their bodies and their inner resources.

Research has shown that, for a healthy woman, labor proceeds normally and without hazard most of the time, and that careful observation is all that is necessary to detect problems in time to take medical action. Actually, one way to *avoid* problems is to be cautious about using optional procedures and medications; these can sometimes *cause* problems: for example, any procedure that restricts the mother's freedom to move might slow labor or increase her pain, thus making further interventions more likely and actually increasing her risk of developing other problems. In sum, technology, medications, and interventions are appropriate and necessary only when problems already exist or are very likely to occur.

Intervention always involves a tradeoff. The mother needs to know what she gives up and what she gains with each procedure. When considering interventions, discuss the following questions with each other and with the caregiver: Is the tradeoff worthwhile?—that is, do the benefits outweigh the possible detrimental effects? Is there a problem that can be solved with the intervention? Are there alternatives?

The next few chapters (6–9) briefly discuss the tests, technologies, interventions (including cesarean birth), and medications commonly used in childbirth, along with the problems they are designed to detect and treat.

6

Tests, Technologies, and Interventions

What constitutes basic care during the labor of the low-risk mother, that is, the mother who is in good general health, experiencing a normal pregnancy, and whose baby is in a favorable position within the uterus? By making certain simple but essential observations regularly during the labor, the skilled caregiver can accurately assess whether the mother and baby are fine or if closer observation or treatment are needed.

Essential Observations

Basic care includes the following essential observations of the mother, the amniotic fluid (the water in the bag of waters), the fetus, and the newborn.

The caregiver makes these observations of the mother:

- Her behavior, activity, and emotional state during and between contractions and after the birth.
- Her basic body functions: eating, drinking, urination, bowel movements.

- The contractions: frequency, intensity, duration, and the tone of the uterus between contractions.
- The mother's vaginal secretions.
- The progress of labor (determined by occasional vaginal exams).
- The mother's vital signs: temperature, pulse, respiration.
- Her blood pressure.
- The tone of her uterus after childbirth.
- The amount of bleeding after childbirth.

The caregiver makes these observations of the amniotic fluid (when the bag of waters breaks):

- The color: red or pink indicates bleeding in the mother; brown or green indicates the presence of fetal bowel movement (meconium), which means the fetus is stressed
- The amount (a leak or a gush): losing a large amount of fluid increases the likelihood of pressure on the umbilical cord during contractions, which could cause stress to the fetus
- The odor: a foul smell indicates infection

The caregiver makes these observations of the fetus:

- The heartbeat, monitored by frequent listening to the fetal heart with a stethoscope or ultrasound device
- The position (which direction the baby is facing) and the presentation (head down, breech, and so forth)
- The size (approximate weight)

The caregiver makes these observations of the newborn:

- The Apgar score (page 125) at one, five, and perhaps ten minutes after birth
- The baby's temperature, respiration, and pulse
- The baby's general behavior and state of alertness

These simple observations, if made frequently by a caregiver who is with the mother continuously, give a very good idea of both the mother's and the baby's conditions. As long as they indicate normal conditions, these observations are all that are truly needed. Continuous contact between the caregiver or nurse, the birth partner, and the laboring mother allows for kindness, expert emotional support, reassurance, and help with pain-relieving measures at all times. It also allows the caregiver or nurse to make other important but less tangible observations about the labor, the mother, or the baby.

Some busy caregivers in busy hospitals rely less on continuous

THE APGAR SCORE

Sign	0 points	1 point	2 points
Heart rate	Absent	Below 100 per minute	Over 100 per minute
Breathing	Absent	Slow, irregular	Good, crying
Muscle tone	Limp	Arms and legs close to body	Active, moving
Reflex irritability	No response to suctioning	Grimace	Struggle, cough, or sneeze
Color	Blue-gray	Body pink or ruddy, fingers and toes blue	All pink or ruddy

contact between themselves and the mother. Instead, they depend on the mother's having periodic contact with a variety of nurses and doctors and on a greater use of technological substitutes (electronic fetal monitors, intravenous fluid pumps, pain medications, or anesthesia).

The two approaches result in about the same proportion of healthy mothers and babies. The difference lies more in *how* these outcomes are achieved. The two approaches can be combined, of course: continuous contact and emotional support can be offered even when technology and interventions are used. This combination is the safest and most effective way to care for mothers who are at moderate or high risk for having problems during labor.

Conditions Influencing the Amount of Intervention

Beyond the essential observations, many tests, procedures, and medications constitute the medical side of childbirth. They involve the use of highly specialized equipment and a variety of drugs. How and when they are used depends on a number of considerations:

- *The medical condition of the mother.* As I have already noted, there is less need for intervention when the mother has had a healthy pregnancy and labor is progressing well.
- *The apparent well-being of the fetus.* If the fetus is fully developed and mature, of normal size, and apparently unstressed, most routine interventions are not needed.

- *The training and philosophy of the caregiver.* Some caregivers routinely use more interventions than others, preferring to treat problems before they arise. Although this practice results in overtreatment much of the time, these caregivers feel that the overtreatment is harmless and that without it they would miss problems. Better safe than sorry, they believe. Other caregivers prefer to reserve treatment until a problem arises.
- *The usual practices or policies of the institution and nursing staff.* These practices or policies are determined by current standards of care, nurses' training, the size and degree of competence of the staff, customs, medicolegal concerns, financial constraints, and other factors.
- *The preferences of the mother.* Within each institution and within each caregiver's practice, there is room for choice. Be sure the caregiver knows the mother's preferences (see discussion of the Birth Plan, page 20); try to ensure that her preferences are central to all of the decisions that are made.

Common Obstetric Interventions

Following are descriptions of many common obstetric procedures and their purposes, disadvantages, and possible alternatives. These are usually optional when labor is normal, but they may become necessary if problems arise. Chapter 7, "Problems That May Arise in Labor or Afterwards," discusses the circumstances under which these procedures are necessary for medical reasons.

As her birth partner, you will be the liaison between the mother and the hospital staff. It is important for you to be familiar with these interventions so that you can inform the staff about the mother's preferences, help the mother make decisions about optional procedures, and help her handle any additional discomfort—emotional or physical—that may arise from the interventions. It is also important for you to make sure the mother understands any changes in the management of her labor that become medically necessary.

Intravenous (IV) Fluids

An intravenous drip is a plastic bag of special liquids containing water, electrolytes, dextrose, or medications. It hangs from a pole attached to the bed or a pole on wheels; the latter allows the mother to walk. A tube extending from the bag is inserted into a vein in the mother's hand or arm. The liquid drips into the vein.

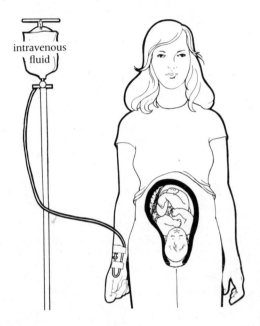

intravenous
fluid

A mother receiving intravenous (IV) fluids.

Purposes of Giving IV Fluids. Intravenous fluids may be given (1) to provide the mother liquids, calories, or both, instead of having her drink them; (2) to administer medications; or (3) to keep a vein open, just in case the mother requires medications later on.

Many caregivers give intravenous fluids to all their patients in labor, because they do not want these women to eat or drink anything. They feel an empty stomach is best. Their reason dates from the time when most women gave birth while unconscious under general anesthesia. It was dangerous for a woman to have a full stomach while under general anesthesia because she might vomit and breathe in the vomited material. The policy of giving all mothers IVs is continued by many caregivers today, even though general anesthesia is now rarely used for childbirth and, when it is, better techniques help protect the patient from this complication.

Some caregivers have a different attitude toward intravenous fluids. They believe intravenous fluids are an unnecessary intervention much of the time, and they encourage mothers to meet their need for fluids by drinking enough to satisfy their thirst. Intravenous fluids are reserved for times when they are ''medically indicated''—that is, when they are necessary or desirable because of the medical condition of the mother or baby.

When are IV fluids medically indicated?

- When labor is very long.
- When the mother has continuous nausea and vomiting.
- When she will receive regional or general anesthesia (page 167).
- When she needs certain IV medications.
- When she has a condition that might require immediate medical action.

Disadvantages of Giving IV Fluids. Besides causing the mother some discomfort and inconvenience, IV fluids, in large amounts, may cause temporary low blood sugar or electrolyte imbalance in the baby. Caregivers disagree on whether this is potentially serious for the baby.

Alternatives to Consider. You and the mother can discuss the following alternatives with the mother's caregiver:

- If labor is proceeding rapidly, do not give the mother any IV fluids; the mother may get along without any fluids, by vein or by mouth.
- Give the mother fluids to drink or popsicles to eat. It is a good idea for her to drink something after each contraction.
- Keep a vein open (in case of emergency) without giving IV fluids. To do this, the caregiver places a needle in a vein in the back of the hand, but the needle is plugged and not connected to an intravenous line. An anticoagulant (heparin) is used to keep a clot from forming at the site. This procedure (called a *heparin lock*) allows the mother more freedom to move around than does an intravenous line. It also allows the caregiver to give intravenous medications very quickly if the need arises. A heparin lock does sting when it is inserted.

Electronic Fetal Monitoring (EFM)

There are two methods of electronic fetal monitoring (EFM), external and internal.

With external monitoring, the nurse or caregiver places two stretchy belts around the mother's abdomen. One holds an ultrasound device in the best place to detect the fetal heartbeat. It is placed low on the woman's abdomen. The other, placed higher, holds a device (a *tocodynamometer*) that detects contractions.

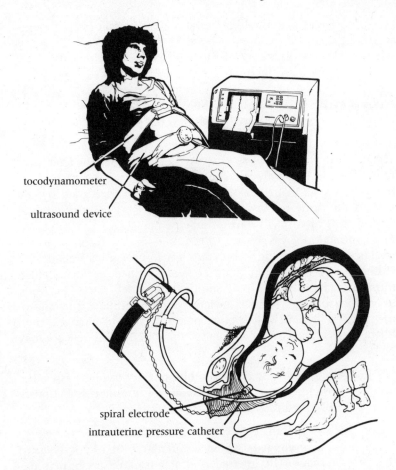

tocodynamometer

ultrasound device

spiral electrode

intrauterine pressure catheter

*Electronic fetal monitoring (EFM): external (*above*) and internal (*below*).*

With internal fetal monitoring, a thin, spiral wire electrode is placed in the skin of the baby's scalp to detect the fetal heart rate. And a fluid-filled plastic tube (an intrauterine pressure catheter) is placed within the mother's uterus to detect and measure the intensity of the contractions. When the uterus contracts, fluid is squeezed out of the tube, and a gauge measures the strength of the contraction. All these devices are connected by wires to a calibrating and recording machine that flashes numbers every second on a digital display, indicating both fetal heart rate and tone in the uterus. These readings are continuously printed out on paper in graph form. Many women and their partners find it helpful to use the contraction monitor as a guide to when to begin patterned breathing and relaxation for each contraction.

The external methods are easier to apply and less invasive, but they are less accurate than the internal methods.

Purposes of EFM. Before labor, EFM is used to assess the fetus's well-being as determined by the *nonstress test* or the *contraction stress test*.

• The nonstress test uses EFM to assess the response of the fetal heart rate when the fetus moves. The mother indicates when she feels her baby move. If the heart rate speeds up, this is a good sign; if it stays the same or slows down, the fetus may be stressed, and further tests or corrective action may be necessary.
• The contraction stress test uses EFM to assess the response of the fetal heart rate when the uterus contracts. Contractions are induced, either with a labor-stimulating hormone (called oxytocin) given intravenously, or with nipple stimulation, which causes the body to produce more oxytocin. If the fetal heart rate remains unchanged, this is a good sign. If it shows certain significant changes, then further tests, corrective action, induction, or cesarean delivery may be necessary.

During labor, EFM is used to help the caregiver or nurse assess the fetus's response to labor and the adequacy of uterine contractions. When is EFM medically indicated?

• When there are doubts before labor about the fetus's well-being.
• When labor is prolonged and a decision about the use of oxytocin needs to be made. The internal contraction monitor can help determine if the contractions are strong enough without additional oxytocin.
• When a nurse or a midwife cannot be with the mother continuously.
• When the mother receives oxytocin or other medications that might affect the fetus.
• When there are doubts during labor about the fetus's well-being (because of prematurity, small size, or possible lack of oxygen).
• When the mother is considered to be at high risk for complications.

Disadvantages of EFM. These are—

• The mother's movements are restricted, although she can change position in bed and sometimes even stand by the bed or sit in a chair. Internal monitoring is less restrictive than external.

- Sometimes more attention is paid to the machine than to the mother. As her birth partner, do not allow yourself to fall into this trap.
- Interpretation of the monitor printouts (tracings) is extremely complex, and experts disagree among themselves about when intervention is necessary and about what different heart-rate patterns really mean.
- Internal monitoring requires both breaking the bag of waters and breaking the skin of the fetal scalp. These procedures slightly increase the risk of infection to mother and baby, especially if the mother has an infection or sore in her vagina. Also, breaking the bag of waters may cause additional stress to the fetus because it removes the cushion of fluid that protects the head and cord.

Alternatives to Consider. You and the mother can discuss the following alternatives to EFM with the mother's caregiver:

- Have a nurse or caregiver listen frequently to fetal heart tones with a regular fetal stethoscope or ultrasound stethoscope for one or two minutes at a time, during and after a contraction. In many studies, researchers have found this method results in equally healthy babies and fewer cesareans; it does, however, require continuous attendance by a nurse or midwife who is skilled in this technique.
- Use intermittent external EFM for ten or fifteen minutes each hour. This enables the mother to move around the rest of the time.
- Use a portable radio-transmission (telemetry) EFM unit. The mother wears the unit on a belt, which allows her to move about freely while information is radioed back to a central monitor at the nurses' station. Find out if the hospital has telemetry units available.

Fetal Stimulation Test

The caregiver performs this simple test either by making a loud noise outside the uterus (the fetal acoustic stimulation test) or by pressing or scratching the fetal scalp during a vaginal exam (the fetal scalp stimulation test). The heart rate speeds up with stimulation if the fetus is compensating well for the temporary decrease in oxygen caused by contractions; the heart rate does not speed up if the fetus is not compensating well. The results of this test have been found to correlate well with the more complex, expensive, and time-consuming fetal scalp blood test, described later.

Purposes of the Fetal Stimulation Test. This test is performed to confirm whether the fetus is truly in distress when electronic fetal monitoring (EFM) suggests that it may be. The test is medically indicated any time fetal distress is suspected, and certainly before a cesarean is performed for fetal distress.

Disadvantages of the Fetal Stimulation Test. There are none.

Alternatives to Consider. The alternatives to performing the fetal stimulation test include the following: (1) relying on electronic fetal monitoring alone; (2) relying on frequent listening to the fetal heart rate alone; or (3) relying on electronic fetal monitoring plus fetal scalp blood sampling (see the discussion that follows). None of these provides an advantage over the test itself; the first two result in more false diagnoses and unnecessary treatment of fetal distress, and the last is more expensive, time-consuming, and uncomfortable for the mother.

You and the mother can ask for the fetal stimulation test whenever fetal distress is suspected. Discuss it with her caregiver in advance, and state your preference for it in her Birth Plan (page 20). Being rather new, the test is not yet used by all caregivers. Prior discussion will give your caregiver time to investigate the test if he or she is unfamiliar with it.

Fetal Scalp Blood Sampling

To perform this test, a sample of blood is taken from a small cut in the fetal scalp and tested for oxygen and carbon dioxide levels, acidity, and other characteristics that indicate whether the fetus is doing well or is in distress. It takes from two to thirty minutes to obtain the test results, depending on the laboratory's efficiency and on its location.

Purposes of Fetal Scalp Blood Sampling. Fetal scalp blood sampling can be used to double-check the results of electronic fetal monitoring (EFM). If EFM indicates fetal distress, scalp blood sampling is done to confirm the diagnosis. It is far more accurate in diagnosing fetal distress than is EFM alone; it helps the caregiver judge whether a cesarean delivery is really necessary.

Many caregivers believe that fetal scalp blood sampling should be *required* before any cesarean delivery is done for fetal distress. The problems with this approach are (1) it is simply *not possible* to do the test in small hospitals whose laboratories are not open twenty-four hours a day, and (2) most caregivers *will not wait* as long as thirty minutes for the test results if they suspect fetal distress.

Therefore, in hospitals that can get *rapid*, accurate test results, fetal

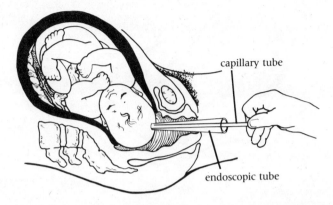

capillary tube

endoscopic tube

Fetal scalp blood sampling. The caregiver inserts an endoscopic tube and places it against the baby's scalp. After making a small incision in the baby's head, the caregiver inserts a capillary tube to draw off a small sample of the baby's blood for testing.

scalp blood sampling is strongly recommended whenever EFM indicates fetal distress. In the case of other hospitals, it is less clear under what circumstances fetal scalp blood sampling should be done.

Disadvantages of Fetal Scalp Blood Sampling. These are—

• The procedure is uncomfortable for the mother.
• The risk of infection or injury to the baby may be slightly increased because of the injury to the scalp.
• The test requires efficient, rapid, round-the-clock laboratory services.

Alternatives to Consider. The caregiver can—

• Use the fetal stimulation test, an excellent, rapid, risk-free test that costs nothing.
• Use EFM alone (but be aware that without scalp blood sampling an unnecessary cesarean for suspected fetal distress may be performed).

Artificial Rupture of the Membranes (AROM)

To rupture the membranes, the caregiver inserts a long thin instrument (amnihook) into the vagina and painlessly breaks the bag of waters. The "waters" (amniotic fluid) come out in a gush or a stream.

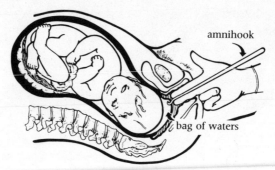

Artificial rupture of the membranes.

Sometimes, following AROM, the woman's contractions suddenly increase in intensity.

Purposes of AROM. AROM is done—

- To speed labor. If timed correctly, it sometimes succeeds.
- To induce labor with or without other methods, such as prostaglandin gel or oxytocin induction (see pages 135–137). AROM is not likely to succeed, however, unless the cervix is very soft and thin.
- To check the waters (amniotic fluid) for a fetal bowel movement (that is, for the presence of meconium, which signals fetal stress), for infection, for bleeding, or for other signs of problems.
- To apply the internal electronic fetal monitor (EFM).

When is AROM medically indicated? This question is controversial. The frequency with which caregivers use AROM, especially in early labor, varies widely. Some believe it is innocuous and use it for most of their patients in labor. Others believe its advantages rarely outweigh its disadvantages; they reserve it for situations where they feel they must intervene. Otherwise, they prefer to leave the membranes intact.

Disadvantages of AROM. These are—

- Frequently, it does not speed labor.
- The chances of the mother or the baby getting an infection are increased if the bag of waters remains broken for a long time before birth.
- Removing the protective cushion of fluid from around the fetal head may increase pressure on the head during contractions and

thus cause more head molding, the gradual and temporary re-shaping of the baby's head that results from pressures within the birth canal. A certain amount of molding is normal and desirable, because it enables the head to pass through a small, tight space. Excessive molding, however, may cause damage to the fetal skull.

- AROM also increases the risk that the umbilical cord will be com-pressed during contractions, which could cause a lack of oxygen for the fetus.
- If the baby's head (or buttocks, if the baby is breech) is high when AROM is done, the danger of prolapsed cord (page 153) increases.

Alternatives to Consider. The caregiver can—

- Refrain from breaking the bag of waters at all or wait before break-ing it to see if labor will speed up on its own.
- Use other methods to check for fetal distress (see "Electronic Fetal Monitoring," page 128, and "Fetal Stimulation Test," page 131) and to induce labor.

Induction or Augmentation of Labor

Sometimes labor is induced (artificially started); at other times a slow labor is speeded up (augmented). There are several ways labor can be induced or augmented:

- Artificial rupture of the membranes (AROM) sometimes speeds or augments labor if it is timed correctly (see preceding discussion).
- A gel containing a hormonelike substance (prostaglandin) can be used when labor must be started before the cervix has softened. The gel is placed within or around the outside of the cervix. It acts directly on the cervix to soften it. Sometimes it starts contractions, too. Doses may be repeated after four to eight hours.
- Intravenous administration of the hormone oxytocin (also called Pitocin) can start or speed up labor. The oxytocin is mixed with intravenous fluids; a continuous intravenous drip causes uterine contractions. By regulating the dose, the caregiver can control the intensity and frequency of the contractions quite well. Electronic fetal monitoring (EFM) is required, along with a nurse's close ob-servation, to detect and correct excessively strong or long contrac-tions. Attempts to start labor with oxytocin often fail when the cervix is firm and thick. If prostaglandin gel is used before oxytocin, this problem is often avoided. If the induction fails, cesarean de-livery is the only remaining option.

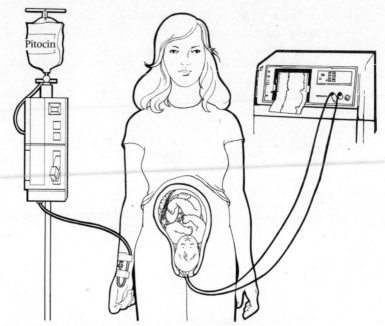

The mother is having her labor induced with Pitocin. Her contractions and the fetal heart rate are being monitored electronically.

Purposes of Induction or Augmentation. Induction or augmentation of labor is medically indicated—

- When pregnancy is very prolonged. Caregivers disagree about when pregnancy has gone on too long, but after forty-two weeks labor is commonly induced. Some caregivers wait for warning signs of problems with the mother or the baby before deciding to induce labor. For these caregivers, the length of pregnancy, by itself, is not a major consideration.
- When medical problems are such that continuing the pregnancy might harm the mother or the baby (for example, when the mother has high blood pressure, diabetes, or one of certain other conditions).
- Sometimes when the bag of waters has been broken for a long time and labor has not started spontaneously.
- When the mother is having a prolonged prelabor and her cervix is firm, in which case prostaglandin gel is sometimes appropriate. (See "Prelabor," page 48, and "The Slow-to-Start Labor," page 97.)
- When contractions in the active phase slow down and decrease in

intensity, causing a delay in progress, in which case augmentation may be appropriate.

Disadvantages of Induction or Augmentation. These are—

- The disadvantages of AROM (page 134).
- Prostaglandin gel has not been approved by the Food and Drug Administration. Therefore, it is not available in all hospitals and the formulas for it are not uniform. Although it has been widely used in Europe for a long time, the safety and effectiveness of prostaglandin gel have not been thoroughly evaluated in the United States.
- Prostaglandin gel occasionally has side effects, such as rapid blood-pressure changes, nausea, and excessively strong contractions. Therefore, it should be used with caution and only after a complete discussion among the three of you.
- Oxytocin-induced labor may be more painful than spontaneous labor, thus increasing the mother's need for pain medications.
- The intravenous oxytocin equipment and setup restricts the mother's movement because it requires an intravenous connection and continuous electronic fetal monitoring.
- Oxytocin may cause contractions that are excessively strong and long (tetanic contractions) and potentially dangerous to both the mother and the baby. If she is receiving oxytocin, the mother's contractions should be closely monitored.
- The baby may be delivered prematurely. Proper timing is very important in order to avoid mistakenly delivering a premature baby. Many babies have been born too early by induction because the caregiver did not know the true due date. Whenever there are doubts about the true age of the fetus, the maturity of its lungs should be checked by amniocentesis—removing and examining a sample of fluid from the bag of waters. The amounts of certain substances from the fetal lungs give information on whether the baby will be able to breathe well if born at this time.

Alternatives to Consider. Instead of having labor medically induced or augmented you can—

- Wait for spontaneous labor. Many caregivers are willing to wait for labor to start on its own—so long as there is careful surveillance of the mother's and fetus's well-being—when the bag of waters has broken, when the baby is overdue, or when the mother simply prefers to wait. If, however, the caregiver feels the baby must be

born soon, he or she will be unlikely to want to "try" an induction, then stop for a few days if it does not work.
• Try the nonmedical methods for stimulating labor contractions described on pages 105–109, "When Labor Must Start."

Episiotomy

An episiotomy is a surgical cut, made with scissors, from the vagina toward the anus. It is sometimes done shortly before delivery. Anesthesia may be given before the procedure, although even if the episiotomy is done without anesthesia, the mother is hardly aware of it. Rather than feeling pain, she is aware of a relief from pressure when the episiotomy is performed. Local anesthesia is given after the birth to relieve pain that occurs when the episiotomy is stitched. The incision usually heals within one or two weeks, although pain at the site occasionally lingers, especially during intercourse, for months. If she still has pain after a few weeks, however, the mother should consult her caregiver.

Purposes of Episiotomy. These are—

• To speed delivery by a few minutes if the fetus appears to be distressed.
• To reduce pressure on the baby's head if the baby is premature or has other problems.

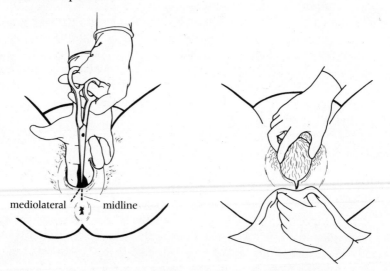

mediolateral   midline

Episiotomy. The midline incision is most common in the United States.

- To try to avoid a tear of the labia (the "lips," or folds of skin, on either side of the vagina) or perineum (the area between the vagina and the anus).
- To allow easier placement of forceps.
- To enlarge a very tight vaginal opening when this is necessary to allow delivery. It is very rare that the vagina will not stretch adequately.
- To prevent permanent stretching of the vagina. There have been no long-term studies to prove whether an episiotomy will prevent permanent stretching. Research indicates, however, that the use or non-use of an episiotomy is less important than a woman's exercise habits and fitness level. See "The Kegel (Pelvic Floor Contraction) Exercise," page 15.

When is an episiotomy medically indicated?

- When the fetus is in distress.
- When a rigid perineum slows and impedes delivery.
- If the caregiver believes the perineum or labia will tear. The likelihood of a tear, in normal circumstances, is a highly controversial issue in obstetrics today. Some caregivers routinely rely on episiotomies; they were taught that the perineum almost always tears badly if an episiotomy is not done. Others seldom do episiotomies; they generally rely on their skills to prevent serious tears, and use episiotomies only for the other indications listed here. The former group perform episiotomies on almost every mother in their care. The latter perform episiotomies on approximately 10 to 20 percent of mothers.
- If the mother's tissues are easily injured (*friable*), as is sometimes the case if she is anemic or has an irritating vaginal infection. An episiotomy in such a case may help prevent extensive damage.

Disadvantages of Episiotomy. These are—

- An episiotomy will *definitely* damage the mother's perineum; she will have a cut, stitches, a healing period, and some discomfort or pain. If no episiotomy is done, however, there is only about a 50 percent chance that the mother's perineum will have a tear. In any case, research indicates that tears are almost always smaller and heal more quickly than the average episiotomy.
- Episiotomies sometimes *extend*—that is, after the cut is made, the pressure of the baby's head can enlarge the incision. This happens in approximately one woman in twenty. Spontaneous tears are

rarely (fewer than one time in one hundred) as large as extended episiotomies. In other words, the chance of a serious tear is greater with an episiotomy than without.

Alternative to Consider. Ask the caregiver to try to avoid an episiotomy, even if it appears that the mother might tear. If the caregiver agrees, the mother may incur no damage, one or several small tears, or, rarely, a large tear. Many caregivers know techniques that protect the perineum from tearing seriously (for example, placing hot compresses on the perineum, controlling the birth of the head and shoulders, massage, spontaneous bearing down). (See "The Crowning and Birth Phase," page 65, and "Spontaneous Bearing Down," page 89.) Furthermore, if the mother has done prenatal perineal massage (page 16), or you've done it for her, her need for an episiotomy is reduced.

In any case, exercising the pelvic floor muscles after birth seems to be more important to the recovery of pelvic floor tone than whether or not the mother had an episiotomy. (See "Perineum," page 206 in chapter 10 for a description of the Kegel exercise.)

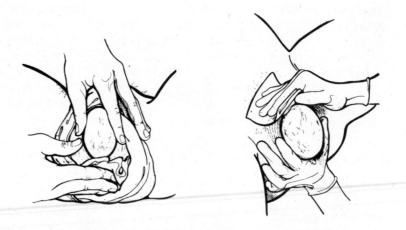

An alternative to episiotomy. Left, the caregiver uses warm compresses to promote relaxation and circulation, and gently supports the perineum. Right, the caregiver provides slight counterpressure as the baby's head emerges.

Vacuum Extraction

Vacuum extraction is used during the birthing (second) stage of labor. A plastic suction cup (about three inches in diameter) is placed on the baby's head; the suction cup is connected to handles and to a device that sets the amount of suction at a safe level. The caregiver pulls on the device attached to the baby's head while the uterus contracts and the mother pushes. The suction cup disengages if the caregiver pulls too hard, thus protecting the baby's head.

Purposes of Vacuum Extraction. Vacuum extraction is done to assist or hasten delivery after the baby's head is in the birth canal. It is medically indicated—

- If the birthing (second) stage of labor is prolonged because fatigue or anesthesia have made the mother unable to push effectively.
- If the birthing stage is prolonged because the baby is large and the mother's efforts need assistance.
- If there is last-minute fetal distress.

Compared with forceps (page 142), the vacuum extractor is less likely to require an episiotomy; it may cause less damage to the woman's vagina; it can be used when the baby is higher in the birth canal; and it appears to be about as safe.

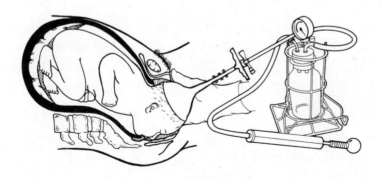

Vacuum extraction. After applying a suction cup to the baby's scalp, the caregiver pulls as the mother pushes and the uterus contracts.

Disadvantages of Vacuum Extraction. These are—

- Vacuum extraction frequently causes a fluid-filled lump on the baby's head where the suction cup was. It may take days or weeks for the lump to disappear.
- If the suction cup pops off during use, both the birth partner and the mother may be alarmed. Remember, it pops off to protect the baby from excessive strain.
- Bruising or more serious injury to the fetal head is possible, though unlikely when vacuum extraction is used properly.
- Most midwives and some physicians are not trained to use this technique, so it is not always an option.

Alternatives to Consider. These are—

- The mother can bear down (push) in different positions, such as squatting or standing. (See "Positions for the Birthing (Second) Stage," page 77.)
- Forceps can be used for delivery. (See below.)
- A cesarean section can be performed. (See chapter 9.)

Forceps Delivery

Forceps are used during the birthing stage: two steel instruments (called *blades*, though they are more like spoons or salad tongs) are placed within the vagina on either side of the baby's head. They are then locked into position and cannot be further tightened on the baby, which protects the baby's head from undue pressure. The doctor pulls during the contraction while the mother pushes.

Purposes of Using Forceps. The doctor uses forceps to deliver the baby more quickly. A forceps delivery is medically indicated—

- If the birth is delayed because (1) the mother is not able to push effectively, (2) there is a decrease in uterine contractions, or (3) the baby is large.
- If there is fetal distress when the baby is low in the birth canal.

If the baby is high, either a vacuum extraction or a cesarean delivery (see chapter 9) are safer choices.

Disadvantages of Forceps Delivery. These are—

- Forceps almost always require an episiotomy and anesthesia.
- Though it happens rarely, forceps may injure the baby.
- The forceps may injure the mother's birth canal.

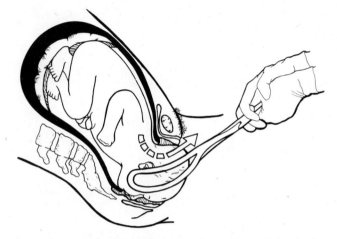

Forceps are placed in the mother's vagina around the baby's head. The doctor pulls while the mother pushes and the uterus contracts.

Alternatives to Consider. These are—

- The mother can use directed pushing in positions that enlarge the pelvis, such as squatting or a supported squat. (See "Positions for the Birthing (Second) Stage," page 77, and "Directed Pushing," page 90.)
- The caregiver can monitor the fetus and the mother, and, if both are doing well, give the labor more time.
- The caregiver can use vacuum extraction. (See above.)
- The caregiver can perform a cesarean delivery if it appears that a forceps delivery would be difficult. (See chapter 9.)

7

Problems That May Arise in Labor or Afterwards

*T*his chapter discusses the most common problems that sometimes arise during labor, how they are treated, and how you can help the mother. These problems usually resolve themselves with time or with minor interventions; but occasionally they require rapid action and major interventions, such as cesarean delivery. The problems fall into four major categories: problems with the mother; problems with the labor; problems with the fetus; and problems with the newborn.

As you would imagine, the mother will be upset—worried, shocked, stunned, frightened, anxious, or even suspicious—if problems arise. She may have difficulty accepting that there is a problem, especially if she feels normal. It is awfully hard to cope with much more than labor itself, and she may rely on you to assume some of the responsibility for decision making.

As the birth partner, you can help in the following ways:

- Learn, and help the mother to understand, what is happening, why it is a problem, how serious it is, and the rationale for and the expected results of any corrective action to be taken.
- Help the mother adjust to the need for a change in management. She may need help making decisions.

- Remain assertive and cooperative with her caregiver. Ask questions, inform the staff of the mother's wishes, and learn of any alternative ways of handling the problem.
- Recognize the need to accept the caregiver's judgment in true emergencies, when time is of the utmost importance.
- Remain with the mother throughout. When things go wrong, she needs your help and support more than ever.
- Afterwards, allow her time to recover emotionally.

Problems with the Mother

Premature Labor

If a woman begins labor before thirty-seven weeks of pregnancy, the labor is considered premature (see "The Signs of Labor," page 36, for an explanation of signs of premature labor). If the baby is born prematurely, he is at greater risk for a number of medical problems, such as breathing difficulties, jaundice, infection, difficulty maintaining body temperature, and feeding problems.

Management of Premature Labor. This depends on the fetus's gestational age, well-being, and stage of development. Measures may include the following:

- A vaginal exam to determine how much the cervix has dilated.
- Assessment of contractions (how long, strong, and frequent they are).
- Attempts to stop labor through the use of bed rest and medications such as magnesium sulfate, ritodrine, terbutaline, or other medications. Bed rest and medications are more likely to be effective if the woman's cervix has not dilated beyond two centimeters.
- Amniocentesis and testing of the amniotic fluid to indicate if the fetus's lungs are mature, that is, capable of breathing without difficulty after birth. This helps the caregiver determine how aggressively to try to stop the labor.
- Electronic fetal monitoring (EFM) to detect contractions and to watch the baby's condition.
- Testing the mother's vaginal secretions or blood for signs of infection, which sometimes causes premature labor. Because infection, if present, may endanger the mother or the baby, the mother must be treated with antibiotics.
- If delivery cannot be postponed, transportation of the mother to a

hospital with an intensive-care nursery, especially if the baby is very premature.
• Summoning of a pediatrician or neonatologist to care for the baby immediately after the delivery.

Rise in Mother's Blood Pressure

The mother's blood pressure is checked frequently during labor. If it rises significantly, this may be a sign that she has *preeclampsia*, sometimes called *toxemia*. Preeclampsia is a syndrome that includes high blood pressure, protein in the urine, sudden swelling of the face or fingers, and, possibly, exaggerated reflexes. If untreated, it may worsen and cause the mother to have convulsions and the fetus to suffer oxygen deprivation (eclampsia). (The management measures outlined here are also used if the woman's blood pressure is high before labor begins.)

Management of High Blood Pressure. This consists of close monitoring of the mother's blood pressure and the other signs of preeclampsia—protein in her urine, changes in her kidney function (as shown by blood tests), and changes in her reflexes. If her blood pressure rises, the following measures are taken to lower it:

• The mother stays in bed, on her left side.
• The mother takes a long shower or bath (now acceptable in only a few hospitals).
• The mother is given medication to lower her blood pressure (Apresoline) or to prevent convulsions (magnesium sulfate). These are usually given intravenously, but they may be given by injection.
• The birth of the baby is hastened by induction, augmentation of labor, or cesarean delivery if the condition worsens to a dangerous level.

Mother's Reactions. The mother may react in any of these ways when told her blood pressure has risen dangerously:

• Since a woman usually feels fine when her blood pressure is mildly elevated, she may find it hard to believe she has a problem, and she may feel irritated by the restrictions on her activity in labor.
• The prospect of having convulsions may frighten her.
• If she receives magnesium sulfate, she may feel hot and flushed, or nervous, and may have discomfort with breathing. Her labor may slow down.

- If she receives Apresoline, she may feel lightheaded. Her nose may become congested.

How You Can Help. You can sympathize with her, but help her focus on what she must do for her own and the baby's welfare. Remind her of those comfort measures she still can use (see "If the Mother Must Labor in Bed," page 111).

Herpes Lesion

On visual inspection, a herpes sore in the mother's genital area may be discovered. Some caregivers rely on weekly cultures of the vagina for women who have had herpes in the past. If the most recent culture was positive for herpes, they assume the woman still has an active lesion at the onset of labor. An active herpes lesion could present a danger to the baby, who may contract the virus during vaginal delivery. Herpes in the newborn is very serious, frequently causing brain damage and death.

Management of Delivery when a Herpes Lesion Is Present. When a lesion is discovered—

- A cesarean delivery is performed to prevent the baby from coming into contact with the sore.
- The baby may be tested for herpes after birth and treated with an anti-herpes medication (acyclovir) if the test is positive.

Mother's Reactions. The mother will probably be disappointed, shocked, angry, or depressed when she learns she has an active herpes lesion, especially if she didn't expect it. If you were the source of her herpes, you may be the target of some of her anger. Expect her to need time, support, and perhaps counseling afterwards to deal with her disappointment over any changes in plans or problems in the baby caused by the herpes.

Excessive Bleeding during Labor or after Birth

Most bleeding comes from the site of the placenta. If the placenta begins to separate during labor, the woman will bleed; the amount and seriousness of the bleeding depend on how extensive the separation is. If the placenta is located very low in the uterus (a condition called *placenta previa*), blood comes out of the vagina. If the placenta is high in the uterus and it begins to separate (*placental abruption*),

Left, *placenta previa;* right, *placental abruption.*

the blood goes into the amniotic fluid and is not seen until the membranes rupture. With placental abruption the uterus may become very firm between contractions, and the mother is in constant pain. Both mother and baby are in danger. This is potentially an acute emergency.

Management of Bleeding during Labor. This complication is managed in the following ways:

- If the bleeding begins late in labor, is not severe, and the fetus appears to be tolerating it, the doctor or midwife monitors the situation and waits. A vaginal birth may be possible.
- If the bleeding begins early in labor (or before labor begins), a cesarean delivery is probable. The mother may receive a general anesthetic if the blood loss is rapid; the anesthetic quickly puts the mother to sleep for the surgery.

Management of Bleeding after Birth. Postpartum hemorrhage occurs for three major reasons: relaxation of the uterus; a retained placenta; or lacerations in the vagina or cervix.

- If the uterus relaxes after the birth, it leaves the blood vessels open at the placental site. If the uterus is made to contract, it will squeeze these vessels closed and the bleeding will stop. To make the uterus contract, the caregiver may vigorously massage the mother's uterus; inject drugs that contract the uterus—Pitocin or Methergine—into the mother's thigh; give Pitocin intravenously; or stimulate the mother's nipples to increase the body's secretion of oxytocin.

- If the placenta or parts of it are retained, the caregiver manually removes the placenta or the placental fragments. This is very painful and may be done under anesthesia. As a last resort, surgery may be required to clean out the uterus, tie off the large blood vessels, or to remove the uterus.
- If there are lacerations in the vagina or cervix, the lacerations are sutured.

The woman may receive blood transfusions if she loses a significant amount of blood.

How You Can Help. Do whatever you are told. A hemorrhage is an emergency, and quick action is essential. There is little time for explanations. If possible, remain with the mother and help her to cooperate in whatever she is asked to do.

The Breech Presentation

See page 113 for a discussion of management of the breech presentation.

Problems with Labor Progress

The caregiver or the nurse regularly observes and records the progress of labor. He or she performs vaginal exams to determine changes in the cervix and in the position and station of the fetus. The caregiver or nurse also observes the quality of the contractions (frequency, duration, and intensity) and the mother's reactions to them. Two situations that may signal problems are *very rapid progress* and *failure to progress*.

Very Rapid Progress

When contractions are exceptionally efficient or unusually powerful, or when the cervix is exceptionally yielding, labor may progress rapidly. A fast labor may be extremely painful for the mother.

Main Concerns of the Caregiver. These are—

- Getting the mother to the hospital in time (or in the case of a home birth, getting the caregiver to the home in time) to care for her adequately.
- How the fetus tolerates the powerful, frequent contractions.
- Damage to the mother's perineum during a rapid birth.
- The newborn's adjustment afterwards. Breathing problems and head trauma may be more likely as a result of this kind of birth.

Management of the Very Rapid Labor. This involves—

- Supporting and reassuring the mother.
- Monitoring the response of the fetal heart to contractions and, possibly, using interventions (changing the mother's position, having her breathe oxygen) to improve oxygenation.
- Attempting to control the speed of delivery by coaching the mother not to bear down and by applying manual pressure against the rapidly emerging head.

How You Can Help. See "The Very Rapid Labor," pages 99–100.

Failure to Progress

We generally expect the progress of labor to speed up by the time the cervix has dilated to four or five centimeters. The cervix is usually quite thin by this time and ready to open more easily, even if it has taken many hours or even a day or two to reach this point (see "The Slow-to-Start Labor," page 97). Sometimes, though, progress does not follow this expected pattern: it may be very slow (in *protracted labor*) or it may seem to stop (in *arrested labor*).

The reasons for a delay in the active phase are more likely to be serious than are the reasons for a slow prelabor or a slow latent phase. It is not always possible to determine why labor is delayed, nor is it possible to know just how serious the delay is until time has passed. The slow progress is not necessarily a concern in itself, but it is likely to be associated with other problems, such as postpartum hemorrhage (page 148), fetal distress (page 155), and inability of the mother to deliver spontaneously.

Cause of Failure to Progress. The delay may result from—

1. *Uterine inertia.* If the contractions slow down and lose their power, the condition is called uterine inertia. Inertia is likely to occur when—

- There is a large baby or twins.
- It is the fifth or later child for the mother.
- The mother has become dehydrated or has gone without food for a long time.
- She is very anxious, fearful, or in great pain.
- Other, less well-understood conditions are present.

2. *Cephalo-pelvic disproportion (CPD) or malposition.* If the fetal head (*cephalo*) is too large for the mother's pelvis, labor will be slowed or vaginal delivery may be impossible. The same is true with malposition. The baby may not be too large, but his head may be coming down at a difficult angle (*asynclitism*), in a difficult position (OP, or occiput posterior), or in a malpresentation (face, brow, or shoulder instead of the top of the baby's head coming down first). (See page 34 for a discussion of presentation and position.)

Assessment of Delay in Labor. The caregiver tries to determine the cause(s) of the delay by assessing the contractions, the size and position of the baby, and the mother's physical and emotional state.

The two possible courses of management are to watch and wait or to try to speed up labor. The choice depends on the situation, the mother's preferences, and the caregiver's philosophy:

1. *The "watch and wait" method of management.* Some physicians, critical of their colleagues' impatience with slow labors, have said,

 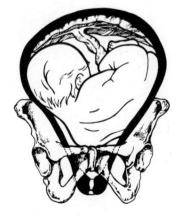

Left, *cephalo-pelvic disproportion (CPD)*. Right, *one form of malpresentation; here the shoulder is presenting first.*

"Failure to progress is really failure to wait." Patience is often the best management when a delay occurs. The caregiver patiently waits while the problem corrects itself, offers support and encouragement in the meantime, and watches the mother and fetus for signs of maternal problems or fetal distress. Although waiting is in the mother's best interests, it may be hard for her, as she may be discouraged or tired. If she is being cared for by optimistic people, however, she will tolerate the wait amazingly well.

While waiting, the mother can—

- Eat easily digested, high-energy food (clear soups, toast with honey or jelly, yogurt, or sorbet) and drink fruit juices.
- Get into the shower or tub. This often relaxes her and reduces the stress that may have slowed down labor.
- Get additional labor support, if possible. The nurse, midwife, childbirth educator, or a professional labor support person may be available to renew the mother's spirits and yours and to help her relax. A fresh face often brings new energy.
- Use body positions to change the baby's position. (See "Backache in Labor," page 109.)

While waiting, the caregiver may—

- Monitor the fetal heart rate more often, or continuously, to help determine if the fetus is tolerating the delay.
- Offer the woman a narcotic, a tranquilizer, or regional anesthesia (an epidural block) to reduce pain and help her relax.
- Start intravenous fluids in the hope that improved hydration and some calories might reenergize the uterus.

2. *The "speed up labor" method of management.* To speed her labor, the mother might try the nonmedical labor-stimulating measures (see "When Labor Must Start," page 105), especially walking and nipple stimulation.

The caregiver may—

- Rupture the membranes (see page 133).
- Use intravenous oxytocin (Pitocin) to stimulate contractions. (See "Induction or Augmentation of Labor," page 135.) Speeding up labor is inappropriate if the problem seems to be CPD or malpresentation.
- Use forceps or a vacuum extractor (see pages 141–143) if the delay occurs in the birthing (second) stage.
- Recommend a cesarean delivery if there is no progress even with the passage of considerable time and after efforts have been made to correct the problem. (See chapter 9.)

How You Can Help. You can help the mother in these ways:

- Suggest the measures discussed here that may help the mother. She may not think of the tub, the positions, extra labor support, the labor-stimulating measures, or the medications.
- Since she may also be reluctant to do things to make her contractions more intense if she is already tired and discouraged, ask another support person to come, or ask the nurse or midwife for help. They may be more able to encourage her to try.
- Be sure the mother recognizes that by trying these measures she may speed labor; remind her that if she does not try them (or if they do not work), she will probably be given intravenous oxytocin and possibly an epidural.

Problems with the Fetus

Prolapsed Cord

On very rare occasions, the umbilical cord slips through the cervix before or during labor. This is a true obstetric emergency, which can result in the baby's death if it is not promptly and correctly managed. The danger is this: The fetus depends on the cord for its oxygen supply.

Prolapsed cord.

If the cord prolapses (slips into the vagina), it can be pinched by the fetus's head or body at the cervix. This obstructs blood flow through the cord and deprives the fetus of oxygen. The fetus can survive only a few minutes without oxygen.

Signs to Recognize. A prolapsed cord is most likely to happen if (1) the fetus is in a breech presentation (buttocks or feet down), or the head is high or off the cervix; AND (2) the bag of waters breaks suddenly (or is ruptured by the caregiver).

With this combination of circumstances, the cord may slip out around the fetal head or buttocks as the fluid escapes; then the fetus, which has been "floating," presses down upon the cord. It is extremely unlikely that a cord prolapse could occur if the fetus has already dropped, or if the head or buttocks are already pressing against the cervix.

CAUTION: In late pregnancy, the mother should ask her caregiver whether the baby is high and floating, low in the pelvis, or pressed against her cervix. If the baby is low, the chances of the cord prolapsing seem minuscule. *If she knows the fetus is high and if her bag of waters breaks with a gush of fluid—*

- She should call for help and call the hospital.
- She should get onto her hands and knees, then drop her chest down to the floor or bed—the knee-chest position (this tilted position uses gravity to hold the baby away from the cervix).
- She should not walk to the car (an ambulance is appropriate under these circumstances).
- If she thinks she can feel the cord in her vagina, she should check with her fingers to see if it is there. She should tell the ambulance team that she has a prolapsed cord and that she should be carried to the ambulance on a stretcher.

Management of a Prolapsed Cord. If the caregiver is present when the cord prolapses, he or she gets the mother into the knee-chest position and places a hand in the vagina to hold the baby off the cord. A cesarean section is performed as soon as possible. With this rapid action, the baby will probably be born in good health.

How You Can Help. Help the mother get into the knee-chest position, and call for help (and an ambulance if she is at home).

Fetal Distress

Fetal distress means that the unborn baby has to adjust physiologically to lower oxygen levels. Although healthy babies have a remarkable ability to compensate for temporary oxygen deficits, brain damage can occur if oxygen deprivation is too severe and continues for too long, or if the baby already has a problem that reduces his ability to compensate.

How It Is Diagnosed. At present, the two best indicators of fetal distress are the fetal heart rate and blood chemistry. They are assessed in the following ways:

- A nurse or a midwife listens to the fetal heart rate with a fetal stethoscope or an ultrasound fetoscope at frequent intervals during labor. This requires that the nurse or midwife remain by the bedside most of the time.
- The caregiver monitors the fetal heart rate, as well as the strength of the mother's contractions, with an electronic fetal monitor (EFM). (See EFM, page 128.)

Remember: If EFM indicates fetal distress, this does not necessarily mean that the baby is definitely in trouble. It may mean only that the baby is compensating for a temporary oxygen deficiency by slowing her heart rate to spare oxygen use. In other words, she may be in trouble, *or* she may be adjusting very well to the decrease in oxygen.

To find out if the baby really is in trouble, the caregiver needs to rely on more than EFM. Tests such as the fetal stimulation test (page 131) and fetal scalp blood sampling (page 132) can help reduce the likelihood of overdiagnosing and overtreating fetal distress. You might check ahead of time to see whether the mother's caregiver uses these other tests before performing cesareans for fetal distress.

Management of Fetal Distress. If monitoring indicates that the fetus may be in distress, the caregiver has these choices:

- Deliver the baby immediately by cesarean, or vaginally, with an episiotomy combined with the use of forceps or vacuum extraction. The choice depends on how close the mother is to delivery.
- Try to correct the fetal distress by having the mother breathe extra oxygen, which is carried via her bloodstream to the placenta and through the cord to the baby, or by having the mother change her position in order to relieve pressure on the umbilical cord that may be causing fetal distress.

- Call for further testing: change from external to internal monitoring, which is more accurate; try the fetal stimulation test; or use the fetal scalp blood sampling test.

Except for the fetal stimulation test, which takes only a few seconds or minutes, these corrective measures and tests take time, and depending on how the EFM tracing looks, the caregiver may be too anxious about the fetus's condition to wait for results. Because this dilemma comes up quite frequently, cesareans are sometimes done that turn out to have been unnecessary.

Mother's Reactions. The mother is likely to react in these ways—

- She will probably be very frightened and shocked when her baby shows signs of fetal distress.
- She will probably not question the caregiver's decisions under these circumstances.
- After the delivery, which may be sudden and frightening, the mother may have very mixed feelings: relief and joy that the baby is all right, confusion about all that has happened, and doubts about whether the cesarean was necessary and about her own behavior or decisions.

How You Can Help. You can help the mother in the following ways:

- Try to keep abreast of what is going on and what the staff is thinking.
- Ask questions. There is little you can do under the circumstances to influence the course of management. If the caregiver is worried that the baby is in danger, you do not want to keep him or her from doing what is necessary. You can ask for the quickly performed fetal stimulation test or for fetal scalp blood sampling as backup to the diagnosis of fetal distress.
- Follow the suggestions given at the beginning of this chapter, page 144.

Problems with the Newborn

The newborn baby is assessed immediately after birth. If all is normal, the baby is usually placed in the mother's arms for cuddling and suckling. If there are problems, the baby will probably go to the nursery for special care. It is beyond the scope of this book to cover newborn problems in detail, but I will list and discuss some fairly common problems that might arise shortly after birth.

If the baby has problems, take part in the decision making about appropriate care. The mother may be unable to think clearly right after the birth because of the effects of drugs, exhaustion, or problems of her own. It falls upon you to become informed and to agree to the course of treatment. Following are some immediate concerns about the baby.

Breathing

Breathing problems may be caused by fluid in the lungs, meconium aspiration (see "Suctioning the Nose and Mouth," page 197), narcotic drugs that were given to the mother inappropriately during labor (see chapter 8), infection, immature lungs, or other problems. A baby who is slow to breathe on her own, or who breathes very fast and grunts as she breathes, may need intravenous feeding, an incubator, deep suctioning, resuscitation, mechanical assistance with breathing, extra oxygen, or other help.

Body Temperature

A baby whose body temperature drops below normal has to use up oxygen and energy trying to maintain it. It is important to keep the baby warm. (See "Warming Unit," page 201.)

Infection

The newborn sometimes acquires an infection while in the uterus or soon after birth. Depending on the organism causing it, the infection may be very serious. Prompt diagnosis and treatment with antibiotics or other medications, along with special care (intravenous feeding, an incubator, and close observation) in the nursery, are needed.

Since infection in a newborn can become very serious very quickly, painful interventions may be necessary. These may include spinal taps, bladder taps, heel sticks, scalp vein intravenous lines, nasogastric tubes, umbilical blood vessel tubes, and apnea monitors. Be sure that you are kept informed, and that there are good reasons to do any of these things to the baby.

Birth Trauma or Injury

Some babies are injured during the birth process, especially if the birth is difficult. A very rapid birth or a difficult forceps, vacuum, or cesarean delivery can cause bruises, broken collar bones, or nerve damage. Although wise management reduces the chances of such injuries, they can occur even with the most skilled caregivers.

For some vulnerable babies (for example, premature babies, babies with defects, babies with preexisting problems) even the normal birth process is too much. Some very large babies also suffer, if great effort by the caregiver is required to deliver them. Vulnerable babies can usually, but not always, be identified before labor, and plans can be made in advance for their special care.

On rare occasions, even with the best of care, a baby is unexpectedly born with serious problems requiring emergency treatment. This possibility haunts parents and professionals alike, but also motivates attempts to develop better diagnostic and treatment methods.

Drug Effects

If a baby is born with a drug in his system, the drug may noticeably affect his behavior. Depending on the drug, he may be sleepy, poor at sucking and breathing, lacking in muscle tone, irritable, jittery, jaundiced, or lacking in some reflex behaviors; or he may show other atypical signs. When the drug wears off, the baby behaves more normally.

The long-term effects on the baby of drugs given to the pregnant or laboring woman are not fully understood. This must be considered whenever a pregnant or laboring woman is treated with drugs. (See chapter 8, "Medications for Pain during Labor.")

Low Blood Sugar

Low blood sugar is rather common in (1) babies of diabetic mothers, (2) very large babies, (3) babies whose mothers received large amounts of intravenous solutions of dextrose in water during labor, (4) babies born after prolonged labors, and (5) babies born under certain other conditions. The diagnosis of low blood sugar is made by drawing blood from the baby's heel and analyzing it. Treatment usually consists of giving the baby some glucose water, formula, or colostrum and rechecking blood sugar levels. The problem usually resolves itself quickly.

Jaundice

If the baby's skin or the whites of her eyes become yellowish, the baby is jaundiced. Usually harmless, *physiologic jaundice* is caused by high levels of bilirubin, a yellow pigment that results when red blood vessels break down as part of their normal life cycle. Physiologic jaundice goes away on its own, usually in a few days. It is thought, however, that high levels of bilirubin in some vulnerable babies may cause brain damage. Premature babies, babies who had particular difficulties during birth, and those with blood types incompatible with their mothers' are more vulnerable to high bilirubin levels.

Jaundice is diagnosed by measuring bilirubin in the baby's blood. Further tests of blood type, liver function, and bowel function help determine the cause. Pediatricians disagree over when treatment should be started: some treat jaundice only when the level of bilirubin is high or rising fast; others treat more aggressively.

Jaundice is treated with phototherapy, which consists of keeping the baby under special bright lights almost constantly for a few days. Light breaks down (photo-oxidizes) bilirubin in the blood vessels of the baby's skin and thus lowers bilirubin levels. Portable phototherapy lights are available in some populous areas for treatment at home. Prolonged exposure to sunlight (preferably through a window) is as effective, though not as reliable, as artificial light. Frequent nursing (more than eight times per day) also helps relieve jaundice.

If the bilirubin levels are very high or if the baby is premature, jaundice is more serious, and a complete exchange transfusion of the baby's blood may be done.

Prematurity or Low Birth Weight

The premature infant (born before thirty-seven weeks' gestation) or the low-birth-weight infant (weighing less than five and a half pounds) is more susceptible to all the newborn problems described here than is the full-term, average-sized baby. Premature babies are therefore watched more closely and receive more aggressive treatment. As they approach average size and weight their vulnerability to problems decreases.

After It Is All Over

I have discussed numerous problems that can arise in both mother and child during labor and the early postpartum period. Each of these presents a challenge to all of you—to the mother, to the caregiver, to the baby, and to you, the birth partner.

Each problem takes an emotional toll requiring quick acceptance of a change in plans and expectations, often without a complete understanding of the situation. At the time, of course, you do what has to be done, even if you are almost in a state of shock. But afterwards, as you and the mother look back over the events, the feelings hit. Even if both the mother and the baby have come through it alive and healthy, the emotional impact can be great. Unanswered questions and feelings of guilt, anger, or disappointment may arise, especially if it all happened too quickly for either or both of you to grasp, or if the mother or the baby was treated unkindly or disrespectfully.

It may take time, especially for the mother, to come to terms with her unrealized expectations. Your patience and acceptance of what is, in reality, a grieving process will help. A conference with the mother's caregiver may help to fill gaps in your understanding of the events and answer questions. Sometimes consulting with a childbirth educator or counselor helps either or both of you to sort out your feelings and gain a healthy perspective on a physically or emotionally traumatic birth experience. Please see page 187, "Your Role during Cesarean Birth," for further discussion of emotional reactions following a difficult birth.

8

Medications for Pain during Labor

Next to the health of mother and baby, the major concern of the caregiver, the birth partner, and the mother herself is the mother's comfort during labor. Although the pain of labor is very intense, it does not have to be overwhelming. There is much the mother can do to keep it manageable. She can learn and rehearse many effective comfort measures in childbirth classes (see "Comfort Measures for Labor," page 73). It is essential for you to help her carry them out; labor is simply too demanding for her to use all she has learned without help.

In addition to nondrug (nonpharmacologic) comfort measures, drugs can be used to relieve labor pain. To a great extent drugs are optional; the mother can decide whether and when to use them. Because they are readily available, and because they can have profound effects, the mother should learn about the available drugs in advance and decide how she feels about using them during labor. You should also be prepared. Do your attitudes toward pain medications match the mother's? Can you agree? Find out in advance how she feels about pain medications, and plan to support her in accomplishing what she wants.

It may seem somewhat foolish for a woman to plan her use of pain medications in advance, since she has no idea how much pain she will feel or how she will react. But she really does not have to know these things to make a good decision ahead of time. Using the information in this chapter, you and the mother can make a plan that will guide you both as you encounter the pain of labor together.

Management of Normal Labor without Pain Medications

The pain of normal labor, though severe, can be successfully managed without the use of pain medications if—

- *The mother wants to avoid pain medications.* Obviously, she is more likely to avoid medications if she wants to. She decides just how important it is to her.
- *She has prepared herself for childbirth.* She needs to know alternatives to medications: comfort measures such as relaxation, patterned breathing, movement, positions, and massage. It helps if the two of you have rehearsed these together. (See "Comfort Measures for Labor," page 73.)
- *She has emotional support.* This is absolutely essential. She needs competent, caring support from you—the person who knows her well, who wants to share the birth, and who wants to help her accomplish her wishes. She also needs the support and help of the professional staff who play a key role in whether she feels confident and capable. A woman in labor is vulnerable to both positive and negative suggestion, especially from those whom she perceives as experts—nurses, midwives, physicians, and professional labor support people. If they believe in her and encourage her, she is more likely to carry on; if they pity, ignore, or discourage her, she is more likely to give up.
- *She has a reasonably normal labor.* This is partly a matter of luck. It must be a labor that does not include problems requiring many painful interventions, one that does not thoroughly exhaust and discourage her. This does not mean labor has to be short or painless. If the first three conditions are present, a woman can handle a long, hard labor very well without pain medications.

If the mother prefers a medication-free labor, prepare yourself well for an active support role.

Pain Medications Preference Scale

It is important for you to know the mother's desires regarding her use of pain medications in labor. You and she should also explore how you yourself feel about her using them. Many birth partners have strong personal feelings on the subject. Some believe deeply that natural childbirth is preferable; some believe that natural childbirth is unnecessary suffering and encourage the mother to take medications. The most important thing is for you each to express your feelings to the other in advance and then prepare together as described here.

You and the mother can use the "Pain Medications Preference Scale" to determine your attitudes regarding her use of pain medications during labor. She rates her desire regarding her use of pain medications. You rate your own desire: Would you prefer that she use pain medications or not? How strongly do you feel? First rate yourselves independently, without consulting each other, by choosing the number on the scale that best matches your feelings. Then compare. If you are more than a few points apart, you will not work as well together as you will if you are closer. Discuss your feelings and come to an agreement. The mother's preferences are more important; you, as the birth partner, help her to deal with her pain as she wishes. Prepare for a support role based on your mutual position on pain medications. The right-hand column, "How the Birth Partner Helps," can guide you in providing appropriate support.

What You Need to Know about Pain Medications

To make an informed decision about pain medications, you and the mother both need some information: What is the drug? How does it work? How effective is it in relieving pain? What other effects does it have—on the mother, on the progress of labor, on the fetus, and on the newborn? Do not wait until the mother is in labor to get this information. When she is in pain and asking for medication, it is too late to try to learn all about the drugs.

Remember that, although numerous drugs are available and widely used in labor, they involve a tradeoff: the mother gets pain relief, but the mother or the fetus may experience unwanted side effects—directly, from the drug itself, or indirectly, through potential problems

PAIN MEDICATIONS PREFERENCE SCALE

Rating	What It Means	How the Birth Partner Helps
+10	• Desire that she feel nothing; desire for anesthesia before labor begins.	• This is an impossible extreme; if the mother says she is +10, she has no interest in helping herself in labor. Help her accept that it is neither wise nor possible to labor without any feeling. The risks make such a choice highly undesirable. She will have some pain and should focus on dealing with it. • Review the discussion of pain medications with her.
+9	• Fear of pain; lack of confidence that mother will be able to cope; dependence on staff to provide total pain relief.	• Follow recommendations for +10. • Suggest she discuss her fears with her caregiver.
+7	• Definite desire for anesthesia during labor as soon as the doctor will allow it, or before labor becomes painful.	• Be sure the doctor is aware of her desire for early anesthesia; learn whether having it is possible in your hospital. • Inform staff of her desire when you arrive.
+5	• Desire for epidural anesthesia (which numbs from the waist down) before reaching transition phase (7–8 centimeters dilation). • Willingness to cope until then, perhaps with narcotic medications.	• Encourage her in breathing and relaxation. • Know the comfort measures (page 73). • Suggest medications to her as she approaches active labor.
+3	• Desire to use pain medications, but not until the mother finds them necessary. • Natural childbirth is not a goal.	• Plan to be active as a birth partner to help her keep medication use low. Use comfort measures (page 73). • Help her get medications when she wants them. • Suggest reduced doses of narcotics or a "light" epidural block (to numb the abdomen only).
0	• No opinion or preference. • This is a rare attitude among pregnant women, though it is not uncommon among birth partners.	• Become informed. • Discuss medications. • Commit yourself to helping her decide on her preferences. • If she has no preference, let the staff manage her pain.
−3	• Preference that pain medications be avoided, but only if labor is short or easy; desire for medication otherwise.	• Do not suggest that she take pain medications. • Emphasize coping techniques, but do not try to talk her out of pain medications if she asks for them.

Rating	What It Means	How the Birth Partner Helps
−5	• Strong preference to avoid pain medications, mainly for the baby's benefit. • Actively preparing (practicing relaxation, patterned breathing and massage and reading outside childbirth class). • Will accept medications for a difficult labor.	• Prepare yourself for a very active role. • If possible, invite or hire an experienced labor support person to accompany and help the two of you. • Learn and practice relaxation techniques, patterned breathing, and massage together in advance. • Know the comfort measures. • During labor, do not suggest medications. • If she asks for medications, try other alternatives: have her checked for progress; ask her to try three to five more contractions without medication; remain firm, confident, and kind; use the Take-Charge Routine (page 94); maintain eye contact and talk her through each contraction; get help from others.
−7	• Very strong desire for natural childbirth, for a sense of personal gratification as well as to benefit the baby.	• Follow the recommendations for −5, but with even greater commitment. • Interpret requests for pain medication as expressions of discouragement and a need for more help. • Remind the mother of how much she had wanted an unmedicated birth. • Only if all these measures fail to calm her and spur her on should you stop trying to help her cope without pain medications.
−9	• Desire that you and the staff deny the mother pain medication, even if she requests it.	• This puts the birth partner in a very difficult position; you will probably feel very uncomfortable denying her medication if the mother is in serious pain. You may even be unable to do it. • Promise to help all you can, but remind the mother that the final decision is not yours—it is hers.
−10	• Desire that the mother forego all medications, even for cesarean delivery.	• This is an impossible extreme. Encourage her to learn about complications that require painful interventions. Help her develop a realistic understanding of risks and benefits of pain medications.

such as restriction of the mother's activity or the need for further intervention. Any long-term effects on the baby of drugs used judiciously in labor have not been established. There may be no harm, or there may be subtle long-term effects. This is a subject of great debate in the medical literature.

For these reasons I advocate using the nondrug methods of pain relief (see "Comfort Measures for Labor," page 73) and reserving pain medications for extra difficult labors or painful interventions. When drugs are reserved for these circumstances, less medication is used, and the benefits seem to outweigh the apparent risks. Most women who plan to use medications in this way derive great satisfaction and fulfillment from participating in and more fully experiencing their children's births.

Several definitions are important in our discussion of pain medications:

- *Analgesia.* Pain relief without loss of consciousness. Analgesics are drugs that relieve pain.
- *Anesthesia.* Loss of sensation, including pain sensation. Anesthetics are drugs that take away feeling.
- *Regional and local anesthetics.* Medications that remove feeling in particular parts of the body, depending on how and where they are given. They do not alter consciousness.
- *General anesthetics.* Medications that remove all awareness and consciousness.

The rest of this chapter presents information about the various medications used during labor. Use it as a guide for making decisions and for seeking further information. The drugs are grouped according to general characteristics. There are subtle differences, which are not described here, among the drugs in each group. The chart "Timing of Pain Medications in Labor," page 180, lists these groups of drugs and indicates at which stages of labor they are most safely given and when their effects will ideally have worn off.

Systemic Drugs

Drugs that affect the whole body—the entire system—are called *systemic drugs.* Systemic analgesics (pain-relieving drugs) use the bloodstream to transport the medication to the brain, where it exerts its pain-relieving effect. Systemic drugs can be given in several forms: as pills, as gases to inhale, or as injections—into the skin or muscle, or directly into the vein.

Systemic drugs circulate not only to the mother's brain but throughout her body; they also cross the placenta to the baby. Because their effects on the baby after birth may be profound, these drugs must be given early enough in the labor to allow time for them to wear off before birth.

Even when the timing is appropriate, some of a drug (or its metabolic by-products) almost certainly remains in the baby's bloodstream after birth and subtly alters his behavior and reflexes for a few days following. How severely medication affects the baby depends on his health and maturity, the choice of drug, the size and number of doses given, and the times they are given during labor. The healthier the baby, the smaller the amount of medication used, and the greater the time between its administration and the birth, the less pronounced the effects will be on the baby.

There are three categories of systemic pain medications that may be given during prelabor or during the dilation (first) stage: tranquilizers, sedatives, and narcotics. Another group of systemic medications, general anesthetics, are occasionally used during the dilation or birthing (second) stage. General anesthetics are discussed as a separate category on page 171.

Regional and Local Anesthesia

Anesthesia (loss of sensation) in a specific part of the body, sometimes called a "block," results from injection of a drug that blocks the transmission of nerve impulses in the injected area, causing numbness and reduced muscle tone. The location of the injection determines not only the specific area that will be anesthetized, but also, to some extent, the side effects.

Although regional and local anesthetics are not systemic medications, they are absorbed into the mother's bloodstream in relatively small concentrations. Direct side effects on the fetus and on the newborn do occur, especially if large doses or repeated small doses are used, causing an accumulation of the drug in the mother's or baby's circulation (or if the medication is inadvertently injected into one of the mother's blood vessels). The greater the total amount of medication, the larger the amount accumulating in the fetus and the more pronounced the side effects. Specific direct and indirect side effects are described here.

There are three major regional blocks: the spinal, the epidural, and the caudal. Each can be given as a single injection, as repeated injections, or as a continuous drip, the last two via a catheter (a thin tube) inserted and left in place. The use of a catheter allows for more prolonged anesthesia than does a single injection.

The spinal block is given in the low back, or *lumbar spine*, through the dura and into the dural space. The *dura* is the membrane that surrounds the spine and the spinal nerves and contains the spinal fluid; the *dural space* is the space within the dura. The epidural block is also given in the lumber spine, but in the *epidural space*, just outside the dural space. The caudal block is given in the sacrum, at the top of the cleft in the buttocks; the medication enters the *caudal space*, which, like the epidural space, lies outside the dura.

The local blocks are given via injection. There are three major local blocks: the paracervical, the pudendal, and the perineal. The paracervical block numbs the cervix; the pudendal block numbs the birth canal, or the vagina; and the perineal block numbs the perineum. The perineal is the one usually called a "local."

General Characteristics of Regional and Local Anesthesia. The drugs used for regional and local blocks are sometimes referred to as "caine" drugs; common examples are Carbocaine, Marcaine, Xylocaine, and Nesacaine. These drugs are quite similar in their effects on the mother, on the labor, and on the baby. Subtle differences in their biochemical makeup, however, affect the way they act in the body and the duration of their effects. The mother's caregiver and her anesthesiologist will select the drugs that are most appropriate to her situation.

In general, the desired effect of the drugs is loss of pain sensation in the area anesthetized. Reducing her pain relaxes the mother and may result in more rapid dilation of the cervix in a delayed labor. Other possible effects (depending on the area injected, the total dosage, and the choice of drug) include the following:

- *On mother:* Toxic reaction; drop in blood pressure; temporary slowing of labor; loss or reduction of bearing-down reflex in second (birthing) stage; need for forceps delivery; spinal headache (with spinal anesthesia only).
- *On fetus:* Temporary changes in heart rate caused by lower maternal blood pressure.
- *On newborn* (depending on the amount of the drug in the baby's blood): Subtle changes in reflexes (other than suckling and breathing reflexes); decreased attentiveness and muscle tone; increased fussiness. These effects seem to last for only a few days.

Technique for Giving a Regional Block. There are many similarities among the techniques for administering the various regional blocks.

The general procedure is described here. Please refer to the table "Pain Medications and Their Effects" for specific information about each type of block.

Regional blocks numb a large portion of the mother's body—between the top of her uterus and her feet. The area affected can be controlled somewhat by the amount and concentration of the drug given and by the placement of the injection. Regional blocks are usually given after the labor pattern is well established. This is the procedure:

1. Before receiving the anesthetic, the mother is given approximately one quart of intravenous (IV) fluids. This helps reduce the chance that her blood pressure will drop.

2. The mother lies on her side or sits and leans forward. An anesthesiologist scrubs the area where the injection will be given, numbs the skin with a local anesthetic, and then injects a test dose of anesthetic between the vertebrae of her low back (lumber spine or sacrum). The test dose helps to ensure that the needle will be placed correctly and also helps to identify an adverse reaction to the drug.

3. If there are no problems with the test dose, a full dose is given. Within minutes the mother begins to feel the effects and is soon numb in the desired area.

4. Sometimes pain relief is uneven or spotty, and it takes some adjustment (changing the mother's position, injecting more doses) before the pain relief is adequate. A thin plastic tube (a catheter) can be left in her back so that extra doses may easily be given, if necessary.

5. The mother's blood pressure and pulse are checked frequently.

Regional blocks may be used for both vaginal and cesarean deliveries. They do not alter the mother's consciousness at all. Administration of these drugs requires a high degree of skill, and is therefore done only by specialists—anesthesiologists or specially trained nurse-anesthetists. Regional blocks are the most costly of all obstetric pain-relieving techniques.

Before choosing regional blocks for pain relief during labor, consider that it may take a rather long time from when the decision is made to use anesthesia until the mother is comfortable. The time involved in preparing the mother, waiting for the anesthesiologist to arrive, administering the drug, and allowing the medication to take effect adds up to thirty to sixty minutes or more. This is a difficult time for the mother; she has decided she does not want to cope any more, and yet she still has to. She may find it harder than ever to wait for the anesthetic to be given and to take effect. You will have to continue encouraging her in breathing, attention focusing, and

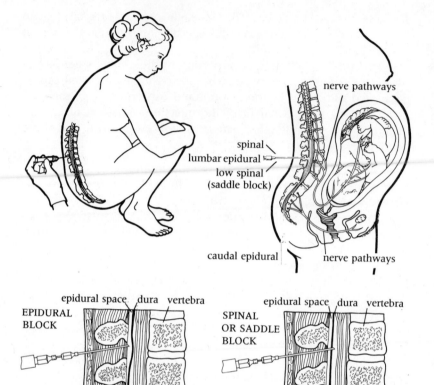

Regional anesthesia. Above left: *As the mother lies on her side, the anesthesiologist injects the anesthetic.* Above right: *The sites of injection for various regional blocks.* Below: *These detailed drawings illustrate the placement of the needle for an epidural block (*left*) and a spinal or saddle block (*right*).*

distraction until she gets relief from the pain. Sometimes, a mother is progressing so fast in labor that she no longer needs the extra pain relief by the time it takes effect. She may be pushing her baby out by then!

Epidural or Spinal Narcotics for Prolonged Pain Relief. A relatively new application of the regional-block technique is the injection of morphine or another narcotic, instead of a "caine" drug, into the epidural or dural space. Through the use of very small doses of narcotics, prolonged pain relief is achieved, usually without altering the mother's consciousness or muscle function noticeably. Sometimes a "caine" drug is given along with a narcotic for combined effects.

Epidural and spinal narcotics are becoming popular for postcesarean and postpartum pain relief. Their use for relief of labor pain is only experimental at this time.

Technique for Giving Local Anesthesia. Local blocks, sometimes called infiltration anesthesia, numb smaller portions of the mother's body than do regional blocks. Giving local anesthetics does not require the skills of an anesthesiologist, because local blocks are easier to administer than are regional blocks. The caregiver draws up the anesthetic into a syringe and injects it into the appropriate sites within or near the vagina. For details about each type of block, see the table "Pain Medications and Their Effects."

Local blocks require larger doses of medication and provide less pain relief than do regional blocks. Also, with a local block more medication enters the mother's circulation; the drug thus affects the fetus and the newborn more profoundly than it would if administered in a regional block. Because of these disadvantages, the paracervical block has almost disappeared from use in many areas of North America, and the pudendal block now tends to be reserved for late second-stage forceps deliveries. The perineal block, or "local," is given either shortly before delivery for an episiotomy, or immediately after delivery for stitching. If the anesthetic is administered close to delivery, the fetus may receive less of the drug and be less affected.

General Analgesia and Anesthesia

General anesthetics are systemic drugs (affecting the whole body). Usually given in the form of a gas to be inhaled through a mask, they rapidly enter the bloodstream via the lungs. They circulate to the brain, where they quickly relieve or abolish the awareness of pain and cause loss of consciousness. Small hospitals rely on general anesthetics more than do large hospitals, especially for cesarean deliveries.

The concentration of the drug determines the degree of pain relief the mother experiences as well as the extent to which she loses consciousness. See the table "Pain Medications and Their Effects" for an explanation of the different effects of different concentrations of inhaled gases.

PAIN MEDICATIONS AND THEIR EFFECTS

Medications	Method of Administration	Desired Effects	Other Possible Effects
SYSTEMIC DRUGS Tranquilizers (examples: Phenergan, Sparine, Valium, Vistaril)	By injection or pill.	• Drowsiness. • Reduction of tension, of anxiety, of nausea, and of vomiting. • Increased tolerance of pain (if used with sedatives or narcotics, tranquilizers may augment the other drugs' effects, so lower doses should be used).	• *On mother:* Dizziness; confusion; dry mouth; changes in blood pressure and heart rate. • *On fetus:* changes in heart-rate patterns. • *On newborn* (depending on amount in baby's blood): increased chances of any of these: breathing, suckling, and body-temperature problems; decreased attentiveness; jaundice; diminished muscle tone (Valium and Sparine cause more pronounced undesirable effects than other drugs in this group).
Sedatives (central nervous system depressants containing barbiturates; examples: Amytal, Nembutal, Phenobarbital, Seconal)	By injection or pill.	• Drowsiness or sleep. • Possible slowing of uterine contractions. • Reduction of anxiety and tension.	• *On mother:* Dizziness; confusion; nausea: nightmares later. • *On fetus:* Changes in heart-rate patterns (barbiturates may accumulate in fetal tissue and remain well into newborn period, having lasting effects). • *On newborn* (depending on amount in baby's blood): Poor suckling; breathing problems; decreased attentiveness.

172

Narcotics or narcotic-like analgesics (examples: Demerol, Dilaudid, fentanyl [Sublimaze], morphine, Nubain, Stadol)	By injection, intravenously, or intraspinally (page 168).	• Pain relief, resulting in relaxation. • Depending on drug used, its dose, and its timing, possible halting of contractions (which may be desired temporarily in a slow-to-start labor [page 97]); because of relaxing effect, possible speeding up of labor.	• *On mother:* Temporary nausea; slowed digestion; dizziness; a "high" feeling; hallucinations; lower blood pressure and heart rate; confusion; respiratory depression; temporary slowing of active-labor progress. • *On fetus:* Heart-rate changes. • *On newborn* (depending on amount in baby's blood): Depressed respiration with possible need for resuscitation; poor suckling ability; depression of other reflexes. Note: As combination drugs, Nubain and Stadol contain narcotic antagonists (see below) and thus cause fewer side effects than the other narcotics listed here.
Narcotic antagonists (a special class of drugs sometimes used after narcotics to diminish their harmful effects; examples: naloxone, Narcan)	By injection, intravenously, or intraspinally (page 168), to mother or baby.	• Reversal of the effects of narcotics if mother, fetus, or newborn is expected to have (or is having) a severe reaction such as respiratory depression, low blood pressure, and so forth.	• *On mother:* nausea; vomiting; sweating; rapid heart rate; increased pain; increased blood pressure; trembling. • *On fetus:* none reported. • *On newborn:* none reported.

Continued on next page

173

PAIN MEDICATIONS AND THEIR EFFECTS—*Continued*

Medications	Method of Administration	Desired Effects	Other Possible Effects
General analgesia with inhaled gases (examples: Ethrane, nitrous oxide, Penthrane, Trilene)	The mother inhales a gas (nitrous oxide or Trilene, in low concentrations) through a mask placed over her nose and mouth. She may administer nitrous oxide to herself during contractions in the dilation or birthing stage. Upon inhaling the gas she quickly becomes semiconscious or unconscious, whereupon the mask falls away and she quickly "wakes up." This "gas and air" method is widely used in Canada and the United Kingdom, not in the United States.	• Very quick loss of consciousness and loss of pain awareness. • Very quick recovery (the loss of awareness lasts about a minute at a time); the medication leaves the bloodstream quickly and has less effect on fetus and newborn.	• *On mother*: Periodic inability to think rationally, or to bear down during birthing stage contractions. • *On fetus*: Little obvious effect when mother self-administers gas. • *On newborn*: Little obvious effect when mother self-administers gas; rarely, possible depression of suckling and breathing.

174

| General anesthesia with inhaled gases (examples: Ethrane, Halothane, nitrous oxide, Penthrane) | An anesthetist places the mask (which gives off a stronger gas than the self-administered nitrous oxide) over the mother's nose and mouth. She inhales it and loses consciousness. Numerous precautions may be taken to prevent the dangerous side effects of prolonged and deep general anesthesia (vomiting and breathing in vomited material); withholding food or drink during labor; emptying ("pumping") the stomach; giving antacids to neutralize stomach acids or medicines to prevent the mother from secreting gastric fluids; and intubating the mother (placing a tube in her throat and windpipe to keep the airway open). This type of anesthesia is reserved for emergency cesarean deliveries, except in hospitals where regional anesthesia is not available. | • Rapid and complete loss of consciousness, which may be maintained as long as necessary to complete a cesarean. This is the best choice when a speedy delivery is absolutely essential for safety of mother or baby (as with a prolapsed cord, page 153, or a serious hemorrhage, page 147).
 • Not as difficult to administer or maintain as a regional block, so people with less training can give it. | • *On mother*: When unconscious, she may vomit and breathe in the material vomited, possibly resulting in serious pneumonia. Unpleasant recovery. Nightmares, confusion. Profound relaxation of uterus which increases the risk of postpartum hemorrhage. Slowing of labor; inability of mother to participate.
 • *On fetus*: Fetal distress due to lack of oxygen crossing the placenta.
 • *On newborn*: Depression of suckling and breathing reflexes; high need for resuscitation; poor muscle tone; grogginess at birth; low Apgar scores. The baby is in a condition similar to the mother at birth. |

Continued on next page

175

PAIN MEDICATIONS AND THEIR EFFECTS—*Continued*

Medications	Method of Administration	Desired Effects	Other Possible Effects
REGIONAL BLOCKS (examples: Carbocaine, Marcaine, Nesacaine, Xylocaine)	See illustration, page 170.		
Spinal block	A single injection, repeated injections, or a continuous drip (the last two via a catheter) into the dural space in the lumbar spine. The mother lies on her side for the procedure. The spinal block is used more for cesareans than vaginal births.	• Short-term loss of sensation (including pain) from abdomen to toes. • Loss of ability to move in the affected areas. • Relaxation when pain is abolished.	• *On mother:* Toxic reaction: drop in blood pressure; loss of ability to move anesthetized parts; spinal headache; decreased ability to push effectively; increased likelihood of forceps delivery; delay in labor, if given early. • *On fetus:* Temporary heart-rate changes caused by lower maternal blood pressure. • *On newborn* (depending on amount of drug in baby's blood): subtle changes in reflexes (other than suckling and breathing reflexes); decreased attentiveness and muscle tone; increased fussiness. These effects seem to last for a few days.

Saddle block (low spinal)	Usually a single injection in lumbar spine (same place as for a spinal). Mother sits up while medication is administered, limiting numbness to a smaller area than in a spinal block. Used occasionally today for vaginal births. Given late in labor.	• Short-term loss of sensation (including pain) in buttocks, inner thighs, and perineum. • Relaxation when pain is abolished.	• *On mother:* Same as for spinal. • *On fetus:* Same as for spinal. • *On newborn:* Same as for spinal.
Lumbar epidural block ("epidural")	A single injection, repeated injections, or a continuous drip (the last two via a catheter) into the epidural space in the lumbar spine.	• Short-term loss of sensation. • In a "light" or "segmental" epidural, diminished sensation (including pain) in abdomen and low back. • In a "standard" epidural, numbness in the abdomen, low back, perineum, legs, and feet. • Relaxation, due to absence of pain; this sometimes speeds up dilation.	• *On mother:* Toxic reaction; drop in blood pressure; delay in progress of labor, especially in a "standard" epidural that is given early; rarely, inadvertent injection of drug into dural space, causing spinal block and spinal headache; diminished urge to push and pelvic floor muscle tone, increasing chances of forceps or vacuum extraction. • *On fetus:* Same as for spinal. • *On newborn:* Same as for spinal.

Continued on next page

PAIN MEDICATIONS AND THEIR EFFECTS—*Continued*

Medications	Method of Administration	Desired Effects	Other Possible Effects
Caudal epidural block ("caudal")	A single injection, repeated injections, or a continuous drip (the last two via a catheter) into the caudal space in the sacrum, at the top of the cleft in the buttocks. Today the caudal is used less, having been largely replaced by the lumbar epidural block, which seems to interfere less with the progress of labor.	• Short-term loss of sensation in the low abdomen, perineum, legs, and feet. • Relaxation when the pain is abolished.	• *On mother:* Same as for lumbar epidural, plus more interference with the birthing stage, due to relaxation of pelvic muscles and loss of the urge to push. • *On fetus:* Temporary heart-rate changes caused by lower maternal blood pressure. • *On newborn* (depending on amount of drug in baby's blood): subtle changes in reflexes (other than suckling and breathing reflexes); decreased attentiveness and muscle tone; increased fussiness. These effects seem to last for only a few days.
EPIDURAL AND SPINAL NARCOTICS (examples: Demerol, Fentanyl, Lofentanil, morphine)	Very small doses of narcotics injected into the epidural or dural space, either directly or via a catheter. Sometimes "caine" drugs are given along with narcotics for combined effects.	• Prolonged pain relief (12 to 36 hours), without noticeable alteration of consciousness or muscle function.	• *On mother:* Nausea and vomiting; retention of urine; itching; spinal headache (if drug is injected into the dural space); delayed problems with breathing (up to 12 hours after the medication is given). The incidence of these side effects is low, but not yet clearly delineated. • *On fetus and newborn:* Unknown, as of this writing, although apparently less profound than with systemic narcotics.

178

LOCAL BLOCKS (examples: Carbocaine, Nesacaine, Xylocaine)

Paracervical block	An injection into each side of the cervix during the dilation stage (before 9 centimeters). Most physicians now refrain from using the paracervical block because of its profound effects on fetus and newborn.	• Short-term reduction of pain (one to two hours) without alteration of consciousness.	*On mother*: Toxic reaction; possible drop in blood pressure. *On fetus*: Marked, prolonged slowing of fetal heart rate. *On Newborn*: Decreased muscle tone; fussiness; inconsolability; diminished reflexes.
Pudendal block	An injection into each side of the vagina, in the pathways of the pudendal nerves, shortly before delivery. This is sometimes used when forceps or vacuum extractor delivery appears necessary (some women tolerate these procedures well without anesthesia).	Numbing of the birth canal during the birthing stage.	*On mother*: Same as for paracervical block. Also, possible diminishing of urge to push and pelvic floor muscle tone, making forceps or vacuum extractor more likely. *On fetus and newborn*: Same as for paracervical block although possibly less profound, if drug is given very shortly before delivery (before maximum dose can reach the baby).
Perineal ("local") block	Several injections into the perineum and vaginal outlet, either shortly before birth for an episiotomy, or shortly afterwards for stitches. The anesthesia is of questionable benefit before birth, as women are rarely aware when an episiotomy is performed. The stretching of the perineum causes a natural numbing.	• Numbing of the perineum.	• *On mother*: Greater likelihood that her tissues will tear due to increased swelling and injury caused by the injection of medicine. • *On fetus and newborn*: If given during labor, same as for paracervical block, though possibly less profound, as the local blocks tend to be given shortly before birth.

Deciding Whether to Use Pain Medications during Labor

In general, whether the mother should use pain medications during labor depends on her wishes, whether she has other ways to cope with pain, and the circumstances of her labor. The particular choice of medication and the amount of pain relief it provides depend mainly on (1) the status of her labor (how far dilated she is, how rapidly she is progressing); (2) the availability of personnel to administer a particular drug; (3) how rapidly pain relief must be obtained; and (4) the degree of pain relief required.

The chart "Timing of Pain Medications in Labor" is a quick guide to the types of drugs available, when they are given, and how long their effects should last. Use the chart and the other information in this chapter as general background for your discussions about pain medications with the mother and her caregiver.

TIMING OF PAIN MEDICATIONS IN LABOR

Medication	Pre-Labor	First Stage 0–4 cm	First Stage 5–7 cm	First Stage 8–10 cm	Second Stage	Third Stage	Post Partum
Tranquilizers	+	+	+	....	....	....	....
Sedatives	+	___	___	....	....	....	....
Narcotics	+	+	___	___	___	....	+
Narcotic antagonists	....	....	....	+	+	+	
Paracervical block	....	....	+	+	___		
Epidural block*	....	....	+	+	+	___	
Caudal block	....	....	....	+	+	___	
Spinal block*	....	....	....	+	+	___	
Epidural and spinal narcotics	....	....	....	....	....	+	+
Pudendal block	....	....	....	....	+	___	
Perineal block ("local")	....	....	....	....	+	+	
General analgesia	....	....	+	+	+	___	
General anesthesia*	....	....	....	....	+	___	

*Can be given for a cesarean at any time, or for a vaginal birth as shown.

KEY

.... Drug effects during these stages are considered undesirable or unsafe.

+ Drug is considered reasonably safe and effective if given during these stages.

___ Drug effects remaining during these stages are considered reasonably safe.

9

Cesarean Childbirth

Sometimes a baby is delivered surgically, through an incision in the mother's abdomen, instead of vaginally. This procedure is a cesarean section, also called cesarean delivery, cesarean birth, C-section or, simply, a cesarean. Today approximately 25 percent of babies born in the United States and Canada are delivered by cesarean. In fact, cesarean section is the most common surgery performed in U.S. hospitals today. Most of these cesareans are unexpected. The cesarean rate has increased steadily since 1970, when it was 5.5 percent, despite the fact that the national governments of both Canada and the United States have convened panels of experts who have studied the situation and concluded that the cesarean rate is too high. Both panels have offered concrete suggestions for lowering the incidence of this surgery. So far, these suggestions have been implemented by very few medical centers, and the rate continues to rise.

Today many women, if they have a choice, seek caregivers whose cesarean birth rates for low-risk women are low. They also choose birth settings in which cesarean rates are low. Additionally, many women concentrate on learning ways to minimize their risk of having a cesarean. Others know little about the rising cesarean rate and are surprised if and when they learn of their odds of having a cesarean.

A cesarean is sometimes necessary and desirable, but it has major drawbacks:

- Usually, it is physically more risky and debilitating for the mother than a vaginal birth.
- The healthy baby often has more difficulty with newborn adjustments after a cesarean than after a vaginal birth.
- Having a cesarean may be depressing or disappointing for the mother, especially if it is unexpected. Most women prefer to give birth vaginally.

Because of these risks and disadvantages, the mother should understand the reasons for the cesarean before it is done and agree that it is the right thing to do. If she finds out in advance that she or the baby has a medical problem that requires a cesarean delivery or makes it highly likely, she can learn all about the surgery and adjust emotionally beforehand. If the need for the cesarean arises in labor, she will have to do much of the adjusting afterwards. Either way, she should have plenty of opportunity to talk about the experience with you, the doctor, and the nurses.

See chapters 6 and 7 for information about problems that sometimes arise in labor and how they are detected and treated; a cesarean becomes the solution if other treatments are unsuccessful.

What if the need for a cesarean arises during labor? If the mother is faced with a cesarean, how can you help? What can you do to ensure that she has as good an experience as possible, even if the labor takes this unexpected turn? This chapter will give you some answers to those questions.

Know the Reasons for Cesarean Birth

What is wrong? Why is a cesarean being suggested? Following are the most likely reasons for a cesarean. Whereas cesareans are not always necessary in these circumstances, they are always considered and very often done.

1. *Emergencies.* These include the following:
- Prolapsed cord (page 153).
- Serious hemorrhage (excessive bleeding) in the mother (page 147).

In these situations there is no time for questions. Rapid action is essential.

2. *Arrested labor.* A failure to progress in labor may be caused by the following:
- Uterine inertia.
- Cephalo-pelvic disproportion (CPD).
- Abnormal position or presentation of the baby.
- A combination of these.

According to many experts, far too many cesareans are performed because of arrested labor. (See ''Failure to Progress,'' page 150.)

3. *Problems with the Fetus.* These include—
- Fetal distress. Many experts believe this is another reason for which cesareans are too often performed. (See ''Fetal Distress,'' page 155.)
- Breech presentation (when the baby's buttocks or feet will be born first), combined with large size and other factors. Vaginal breech births are recommended in many cases as long as the doctor has been trained in the techniques. (See ''If the Baby Is Breech,'' page 113.)
- Prematurity, postmaturity (when the baby is overdue), or other conditions that might make vaginal birth too stressful to the fetus. Through fetal movement counting (by which the mother keeps track of how much the fetus moves [page 18]), nonstress testing (page 130), and ultrasound (the use of soundwaves to obtain pictures of the insides of the fetus), the caregiver determines whether the fetus can tolerate labor.

4. *Problems with the mother.* These include—
- Serious illness (such as heart disease, diabetes, or preeclampsia) or injury. Sometimes, in these cases, a cesarean section is planned in advance. Otherwise a ''trial of labor'' is allowed. The mother is watched carefully and, if all goes well, she gives birth vaginally. If the problem worsens, she has a cesarean.
- A herpes lesion (page 147).
- Infection.
- A previous cesarean delivery. Most women in the United States and Canada who have had a cesarean before will have another, with little consideration of whether they truly need one. This trend contradicts numerous research findings and the government panels, all of which have stated that very few pregnant women who have had cesareans should plan for repeat cesareans. Almost all of these mothers and babies would benefit from labor, and most of these women could give birth vaginally. (See ''The Woman Who Has Had a Previous Disappointing Birth Experience,'' page 115.)

Know What to Expect during Cesarean Birth

You may be surprised by how quickly the staff moves once the decision is made to do a cesarean, and by the number of people involved: there is the doctor who will do the surgery; an assisting doctor or midwife; a "scrub nurse," who gives instruments to the doctor; a "floating nurse," who prepares the room and looks after the surgical team; an anesthesiologist; a nursery nurse to look after the baby; and possibly a pediatrician, if problems with the baby are anticipated. They all work together as an efficient, businesslike team.

You may feel frightened and worried for the mother or baby, especially if they are your loved ones. You may feel relieved to know that the end is in sight, especially after a long, difficult labor. You may be impressed and reassured by the teamwork and competence of the staff. You may feel alone and shocked by their apparently casual attitude. They may talk and even joke among themselves, paying little attention to you and the mother, as if you are not there. You may feel overwhelmed by the sounds, smells, and sights of the surgery. You may be confused over your role. Should you ask questions, and try to make sure that the mother's wishes are being followed, or should you stay out of the way and let them proceed in their customary manner? Just a few minutes before, your role was essential to the mother's ability to handle her contractions; now you feel much less important. The following descriptions of the surgery and of your role will help you to help the mother.

Preparations for Surgery

Preparations for cesarean delivery include the following steps:

- The mother signs a consent form.
- A nurse starts intravenous (IV) fluids in the mother's arm, which is placed on a board that extends out to the side. The nurse checks the mother's blood pressure frequently.
- An anesthesiologist, nurse-anesthetist, or obstetrician gives the anesthetic (spinal, epidural, or general; see chapter 8). The choice of anesthesia depends on the mother's situation (general anesthesia, being fastest, is chosen if the cesarean must be done immediately), the training and qualifications of the staff, and the facilities. Regulating bodies require that hospitals be able to provide general anesthesia, but not necessarily regional anesthesia, around the clock. The mother's preferences also play a role in the decision on anes-

thesia. She should be sure her caregiver knows in advance if she wants to remain awake for a cesarean.

The mother will probably receive oxygen, administered with a face mask.

- Electrocardiogram (EKG) leads are placed on her chest. These keep track of the mother's heart rate throughout the surgery.
- The mother's body is draped so that only her abdomen can be seen. The drape is raised to form a screen between her head and her abdomen.
- Most hospitals now welcome the mother's birth partner (one or more) in the operating room for a cesarean. You sit on a stool at her head. The anesthesiologist remains at her head also.
- Some birth partners watch and even photograph the surgery; others do not want to. Discuss this option with the mother and her caregiver if it interests you. If you remain sitting on the stool, you will see nothing. You have to stand up and look over the drape in order to see the surgery.
- The mother's abdomen is scrubbed and shaved. Some pubic hair is usually removed.
- A catheter is placed in her bladder to keep it empty.

Surgery Begins

This is how a cesarean delivery starts:

- The doctor makes the incisions with a scalpel.
- The skin incision is usually low and horizontal, or transverse (this is called a "bikini incision"), but may be vertical and in the mid-abdomen.
- The muscles of the abdomen are not cut; the fibers are separated and spread apart. The muscles therefore heal very well.
- The uterine incision is usually horizontal (transverse) in the lower segment, but it can be made higher if speed is essential or if the higher opening is needed to get the baby out (for example, in the case of twins or an unusual presentation).
- The amniotic fluid is suctioned from the uterus. You will hear the sucking sound.
- Bleeding blood vessels are tied or cauterized. You may hear the hiss or high-pitched tone of the cautery device or notice a slight odor as it burns the ends of the blood vessels to close them. The mother cannot feel this.

The Baby Is Born

This is how the baby is delivered:

- The baby is usually delivered within ten or fifteen minutes after the surgery has begun. The doctor places one hand in the uterus; with the other hand the doctor pushes on the mother's abdomen. The doctor removes the baby. The mother may feel pressure and tugging at this time. If it is painful for her, help her to use relaxation and patterned breathing (page 85), and ask the doctor or anesthesiologist if she can have more anesthetic.
- The doctor or nurse suctions the baby's airways, and clamps and cuts the cord. The baby may be briefly held up for you both to admire, and then he is taken to an infant-care area in the corner of the delivery room for evaluation. By this time he is probably crying lustily. You may wish to go over and take a look at the baby.
- The oxygen mask is removed from the mother's face.

The Placenta Is Removed
and the Uterus Is Inspected

After the baby is born, the doctor completes the delivery:

- The doctor reaches into the uterus, scoops the placenta from the wall of the uterus, and removes it.
- The doctor then lifts the uterus out of the abdomen to check it thoroughly. The mother may feel this as uncomfortable pressure. She may feel nauseated and vomit, turning her head to the side and using the basin that you or the anesthesiologist holds for her.

The Repair Begins

The repair phase takes about thirty or forty-five minutes. These procedures are involved:

- The uterus and other internal layers are sutured with absorbable suture thread.
- The skin is closed with stitches or stainless steel clips. You may hear the clicking of the stapler as the clips are placed.
- A bandage is applied over the incision.

  Since the mother may be very shaky, trembling all over, or nauseated, she might be given a relaxing, sleep-inducing medication via her IV tube—without either of you knowing about it. If it is important to her to be awake after the birth so she can experience the first hours with her baby, you should ask that these medications not be given without first checking with her. The nausea and trembling usually subside within a half hour.

- The mother is cleaned up and taken to the recovery area. Most hospitals have a multi-bed recovery room; others simply return a woman to her labor room after a cesarean.

The Recovery Period

This is what you can expect during the recovery period:

- The mother remains in recovery for a few hours, until it is clear that she is recovering well and that the anesthetic is wearing off as expected.
- The nurse frequently checks the mother's pulse, temperature, blood pressure, uterine tone, and state of anesthesia.
- You should stay. The baby may be there also.
- The mother can breastfeed the baby now. Ask the nurse to help her position the baby. It is a good idea to start before the anesthesia wears off. It is a little easier for her to get started if she is not in pain the first time. She may need your help in holding the baby up to the breast.
- If she is asleep or groggy from the medication for nausea and trembling, it will be hard for her to nurse. This is why some women refuse the medication, preferring to put up with nausea and trembling for a half hour or an hour: they do not want to miss the first few hours with the baby.
- If she is unable to nurse or hold the baby, you take him. Hold the baby close and talk to him.
- The nurse checks the baby's breathing, skin color, temperature, and heart rate frequently.
- Once the anesthesia wears off and the mother's condition is stable, she is taken to her postpartum room, where she will stay until she goes home. See chapter 10 for information about the first few days after birth.

Your Role during Cesarean Birth

Few women prefer to give birth by cesarean. For most it is unexpected and disappointing, even when they know the surgery has made possible the birth of a healthy baby. Some get over these feelings quickly; others do not. A woman often needs time afterward to adjust emotionally, to talk about and even grieve over the experience, especially if she had a strong desire to give birth vaginally. It is sometimes surprising to loved ones, nurses, and caregivers how deeply disappointed some mothers are. Your partner may need much patience and understanding from you to help her come to terms with her baby's cesarean birth.

The mother is less likely to grieve for a long time if she has been able to participate thoroughly in her labor and in the decision to have a cesarean. Prolonged anger, depression, or guilt may come if the mother is caught by surprise and can do nothing to help herself or make decisions. How you respond to the mother, both during and after the cesarean, also makes a big difference in how well she adjusts. Here are some guidelines:

• Your perceptions of what has happened will be very important to the mother as she puts the pieces together. You can help her come to terms with the experience later if, during the surgery, you stay with her, ask questions, hold her hand, and try to keep her posted on what is happening. You may want to take some pictures; many women treasure them later, especially if they were asleep during the surgery. Photographs help to fill her in on the parts she missed. Whereas she may or may not be interested in photos of the surgery, early pictures of her baby will probably mean a great deal to her.

• The mother, if awake, will probably feel some discomfort during the surgery. If it is more than pressure or tugging, ask that she be given more anesthetic. You should help her continue her relaxation and patterned breathing to handle the sensations of pressure and tugging.

• After birth, do as much as you can with the baby. If possible, hold the baby where the mother can see, touch, or kiss him. Help her breastfeed in the recovery room. If the baby has to go to the nursery for special care, you may want to go along so that you can see for yourself what is being done and fill in these gaps for the mother later. Or, the mother may want you to stay with her.

It may take the mother longer to recover emotionally than it takes her to recover physically. It will also surely take her longer than it takes you. Be patient. Give her time, and help her to understand what has happened.

• Physical recovery takes a matter of weeks or months. Pain, weakness and fatigue are great at first, but diminish steadily for the first week or two. Then, it may take months for the last step—from functioning fairly well to returning to how she was before she became pregnant.

- Women vary in how long it takes them to integrate and accept the cesarean birth experience. For some, a cesarean will be a positive experience; for others it will not be. If the mother is disappointed, accept her feelings as valid and normal. Too often a woman's loved ones try to distract her from thinking about the birth by pointing out that "all that matters" is that she has a healthy baby. But that is not all that matters. Her feelings also matter, and her loved ones' patience, acceptance, and concern for these feelings will help her work through them.
- If the mother's birth experience was particularly negative, she may benefit from professional counseling or therapy. Call her caregiver or childbirth educator for referrals.
- See page 144 for more suggestions about the birth partner's role when problems arise during labor.

Despite her possible disappointment with the birth experience, the mother will rejoice in her baby. A cesarean birth is, after all, a birth, and all the emotions that come with birth also come with cesarean birth. The mother's ability to love, feed, enjoy, and care for her baby are not altered by the fact that the baby was born by cesarean. You will enjoy this child together.

Part Four

AFTER
THE BIRTH

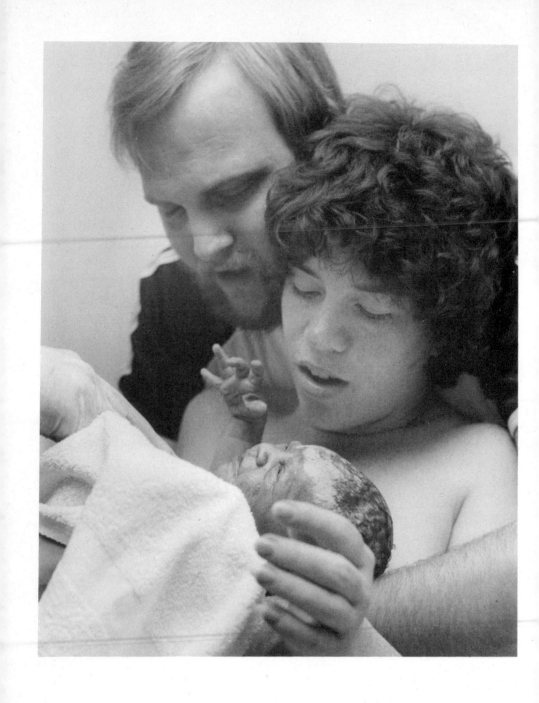

ONCE THE BABY AND THE PLACENTA ARE BORN, THE PACE seems to slow down. Everyone relaxes. The caregiver and the staff seem preoccupied with finishing the medical tasks and with cleaning up. You, the mother, and the baby are almost in your own world, engrossed with the appearance, the touch, the smell of each other. The baby's every gurgle, every grimace, every squirming stretch brings fascinated exclamations and surprised looks from both of you. Some babies are quiet, calm, and alert, drinking in all the new sights and sounds, the most captivating being your faces and your voices. Other babies fuss and cry a lot at first as they discover themselves in strange new surroundings. They seem to need soothing and reassurance right away.

If you are the father of the baby or the mother's life partner, this is the beginning of a "honeymoon" for the three of you. What happens is much like a honeymoon between lovers: withdrawal from the everyday events of the world, intense preoccupation and fascination with each other, profound feelings of love, lack of sleep, and deep contentment.

If your involvement with the mother is as a labor support person only, your contact with her may not extend beyond the birth and a few hours afterward. Make sure the mother has someone else with her during this adjustment period, because she still needs help. You might want to pass this book along to the "at home" support person(s). Chapters 10 and 11, which follow, have some helpful information about the postpartum period and breastfeeding.

10

The First Few Days Post Partum

*D*uring the first few days after the birth, there is much going on physically, medically, and emotionally with both the mother and the baby. This chapter explains what to expect in the first few hours and days—what the caregiver does, what happens with the mother and baby, and your role in all this. Your primary role, of course, is to stay with the mother and give her as much emotional support and practical help as possible.

The First Few Hours

Immediately after the birth, the baby is quickly checked, and (assuming all is well) dried, wrapped warmly, and placed in the mother's arms or in yours. Sometimes the mother holds the naked baby skin to skin, and both are covered with warm blankets. The baby may be crying or may be accustoming herself quietly to her new surroundings. You and the mother will probably be focused completely on the baby, except when reality reenters in the form of the caregiver's or nurse's necessary intrusions. Their agenda is a little different from yours: their main concerns are the physical well-being of the mother and the baby. So, while the two of you are engrossed in the baby, they are dealing with the following immediate clinical concerns.

The Mother's Vagina and Perineum

After a vaginal birth the caregiver carefully inspects the mother's vagina and perineum to determine whether stitches are necessary. This examination is often quite painful if the mother has had no anesthesia. An episiotomy (page 138) or a sizeable tear will require stitches. The caregiver gives the mother a local anesthetic if she needs stitches and if she is not already anesthetized. The stitches are gradually absorbed as the incision heals; they do not have to be removed.

After a Cesarean

After a cesarean birth (described in chapter 9), the mother leaves the operating room and spends a few hours in the recovery room while the anesthetic wears off. She may be very sleepy, depending on the drugs she has been given. There will be a nurse close by all the time. You can remain with the mother, and unless the baby has a problem that requires care in the nursery, he or she can probably stay too.

The Mother's Uterus

The body of the uterus (the fundus) is checked frequently by the nurse to be sure it is contracting tightly. If it is soft and relaxed it bleeds too much. There are three ways to make it contract:

- *Nipple stimulation.* When the baby suckles, the hormone oxytocin is released, which makes the uterus contract. If the baby is not ready to suckle, you or the mother can stroke or roll the mother's nipples, which has almost the same effect.
- *Fundal massage.* The nurse or the midwife does this, but the mother can learn to do it, too. This massage involves firmly kneading the low abdomen until the uterus contracts to the size and consistency of a large grapefruit. This is painful for the mother, which is one reason she should learn to do it herself: she can do it less vigorously and get the same results.
- *Injection or intravenous administration of Pitocin or Methergine.* This is the most reliable way to contract the uterus; it may be used along with the methods described above, although it is not needed in most cases.

The Mother's and Baby's Vital Signs

The caregiver frequently checks the vital signs (pulse, respiration, temperature, and blood pressure) of the mother and the baby, as well as performing other routine assessments. Of course, if the mother or the baby had medical problems during the pregnancy or labor, the nurse or caregiver watches them even more closely.

Common Procedures in Newborn Care

In the first few minutes or hours after birth, the newborn is examined and a number of procedures are done. Many of these are routine; others are optional; some are required by law to detect or prevent certain serious conditions. Because the mother may be exhausted or preoccupied with the things that are still happening to her, it will be up to you to keep track of what is being done to the baby, remind the staff of how the mother wants the baby cared for, and help the mother make decisions, if necessary.

Suctioning the Baby's Nose and Mouth. There are two ways to suction the baby's airway:

1. The tip of a rubber bulb syringe is inserted into the baby's nostrils and mouth to suck mucus, amniotic fluid, or blood from the baby's airway. This is done as soon as the head is out or when the baby is born. Most caregivers do this to all newborns in their practice because it is quick and simple and seems to have few harmful side effects. Some, however, wait to see if the baby needs it.

2. Sometimes, deeper suctioning is done with a long tube that is passed through a nostril and down the baby's trachea (windpipe).

Purposes of Suctioning. Suctioning is done to clear the airway of secretions, especially if the baby is unable to cough or sneeze to remove them, or to assist the baby who is not breathing.

Deeper suctioning may be done if the baby has had a meconium bowel movement while still in the uterus, to keep the baby from breathing the meconium into the lungs. Because the meconium may be in the airway, the caregiver tries to suction it out before the baby's first breath, and again as soon as possible after the birth. New evidence suggests, however, that this procedure may fail to prevent meconium from entering the lungs.

Disadvantages of Suctioning. These are (1) brief discomfort and stress for the baby, who may flinch or struggle when it is done; and (2) possible abrasions of mucous membranes in the baby's nose and throat if the tip scrapes them.

Alternatives to Consider. You and the mother can ask the caregiver to withhold suctioning unless the baby is unable to rid his airway of secretions. If suctioning is necessary, the caregiver can use the syringe gently.

Eye Medications. Medications are placed in the baby's eyes within the first hour after birth. The medications used are either an antibiotic ointment (usually erythromycin) or silver nitrate drops.

Purposes of Eye Medications. These medications prevent serious eye infection or even blindness due to bacteria that cause gonorrhea or chlamydia, two common sexually transmitted diseases. These bacteria are sometimes present in the vagina and can be transmitted to the baby during birth. Silver nitrate protects against gonorrhea only; erythromycin protects against both gonorrhea and chlamydia.

Eye medication is medically indicated if the mother tests positive for chlamydia or gonorrhea or if either parent may have been exposed to the diseases (by having sex with someone else). Because lab tests can miss these infections, medication is required by all states and provinces unless the parent refuses it and the nurse (or other person required to give it) agrees to withhold it from the baby.

Disadvantages of Eye Medications. They temporarily blur the baby's vision. Additionally, silver nitrate irritates the eyes and appears to burn.

Alternatives to Eye Medications. You and the mother might request erythromycin rather than silver nitrate, because the antibiotic is not painful and is less irritating. Or you can refuse any eye treatment, but this may be risky because the organisms, especially chlamydia, are very prevalent and are not always tested for. Chlamydia or gonorrhea organisms may not cause symptoms in adults and therefore sometimes go untreated and spread to the baby. Unfortunately, the newborn can be seriously infected by these organisms. Your nurse or caregiver may feel very uncomfortable if you refuse, since many states hold the caregiver responsible if eye treatment is not given and the baby develops one of these infections.

Vitamin K. An injection or oral dose of vitamin K is given within an hour after birth. This vitamin is essential in the clotting of blood. Newborns are relatively slow in clotting their blood for the first week or so, although once they start eating and digesting food they begin making their own vitamin K. Until then, they are at added risk for excessive bleeding (called *hemorrhagic disease of the newborn*). Giving them vitamin K to tide them over reduces the risk of bleeding problems.

Most hospitals and doctors give vitamin K only by injection, because giving it my mouth has only recently been approved by the American Academy of Pediatrics and the Canadian Paediatric Society. The injection must be used if the baby spits out the oral dose or if she needs to have her stomach emptied as part of an emergency treatment.

Purposes of Giving Vitamin K. The vitamin is given—

- Whenever internal bleeding is more likely than usual, as in a difficult or forceps birth.
- When the baby is premature.
- When circumcision or other surgery is planned before the baby is a week old.
- Routinely in the United States and Canada, because it is quick, easy, and inexpensive to give, and very effective in preventing hemorrhagic disease.

Disadvantages of Giving Vitamin K. These are—

- The injection is painful.
- Administered orally, it does not taste good and has to be given carefully to be sure that the baby swallows it.
- Large doses of vitamin K have been associated with newborn jaundice (see page 158).

Alternatives to Giving Vitamin K. You and the mother may ask the hospital, your baby's doctor, or your midwife for the less traumatic oral administration of vitamin K. Refusing vitamin K altogether is a risky option, because it is not possible to predict which babies will or will not develop hemorrhagic disease.

Blood Tests

Blood samples are obtained in two ways.

A few drops of the baby's blood are drawn from the heel to check for—

- The level of bilirubin, a yellowish blood pigment that at high levels causes jaundice.
- Blood sugar (glucose) levels.
- Two rare disorders that cause mental retardation if left untreated: PKU (phenylketonuria), and congenital hypothyroidism. Low levels of particular substances in the blood indicate these disorders.

Blood from the baby's umbilical cord may also be collected at birth for—

- Blood typing.
- Rh determination.
- The Coombs Test, if the mother is Rh-negative. This tells if the baby's Rh-positive red blood cells are being destroyed by antibodies against the Rh factor that may have crossed from the mother's bloodstream to the baby's. If so, immediate treatment is necessary.

Purposes of Blood Tests. The general purpose of testing the newborn's blood is to detect potentially serious problems early enough to treat them and prevent dangerous effects on the baby.

The PKU test is required for all babies in North America. If the first test indicates PKU, a second test is done, and, if appropriate, a special diet is prescribed.

Other tests may be performed if the baby is at risk for any of certain disorders, as determined by family history and the course of the pregnancy or the postpartum period.

Disadvantages of Blood Tests. The heel stick is painful to the baby, and some of the tests (such as those for bilirubin and blood glucose) may have to be repeated many times.

Also, results of blood tests are sometimes confusing and can lead to overtreatment. Experts sometimes disagree on the interpretation of the results and the appropriate course of action. For example, the question of when bilirubin and blood glucose levels are dangerous is the subject of great controversy. For years babies were treated for jaundice when their bilirubin levels were only slightly elevated. As we have learned more, we have begun reserving treatment for the relatively few babies with rather high levels.

Alternatives to Consider. You and the mother can ask the caregiver about less painful ways to gain the information provided by blood tests. For example, you can observe the baby's skin and the whites of his eyes, and do a blood test for jaundice only if they appear yellow. Weigh the risks and benefits of the recommended test and the problem it is designed to detect, and then make informed choices.

If a blood test shows a problem requiring treatment, such as jaundice or low blood sugar (*hypoglycemia*), you can seek a second opinion. If the second caregiver interprets the test results in the same way as the first, you may be reassured that treatment is necessary. If the two opinions disagree, you and the mother can follow the one that makes the most sense to you.

Warming Unit. A warming unit is a special bed with a heater above it. A baby who is placed in a warming unit has a small thermostat taped to her abdomen; the thermostat automatically turns up the heat if the baby gets chilled. Small or premature babies get chilled more easily than average-size or full-term babies.

Purposes of the Warming Unit. The unit is used to prevent a temperature drop and its harmful aftereffects (sluggishness, increased blood sugar, lung problems, and others), or to warm a baby who has become chilled.

Disadvantages of the Warming Unit. The baby is separated from her parents. Also, warming units are not risk-free; they cause the baby to lose fluids. This fluid loss must be monitored carefully, and the fluids replaced.

Alternatives to Consider. To prevent chills, dry the baby right after the birth and don't leave her exposed to the air. Keep her warm by placing her skin-to-skin against her mother and covering her with a hat and blanket, or wrapping her snugly in a warm blanket.

Cleanup

The mother's bed is changed; the caregiver or the nurse helps the mother wash up and put on a clean gown. The mother should make sure the gown opens in the front for convenience in breastfeeding. The mother wears a sanitary napkin to catch the bloody vaginal discharge (called lochia) which will be present for several days or weeks. The baby is wiped clean, dressed, and diapered. The baby should wear a hat (which you or the hospital supplies). A hat helps keep the baby warm all over; when his head is uncovered, heat is lost from his entire body.

During all this clean-up activity, the mother should hold the baby close to her breast so that he can nurse as soon as he is ready. The nurse or the midwife can be a great help in getting the baby to "latch on" to the breast correctly. Ask for help if the baby is having difficulty or if the mother is unsure of what to do. See chapter 11 for more on breastfeeding.

When the immediate postpartum care is over, the mother, the baby, and the birth partner are often left alone for a while in peace and quiet. Dim the lights to encourage the baby to open his eyes; enjoy these quiet moments together. You and the mother both will soon be ready for a meal. If the mother had a cesarean delivery, it might be some time before she is offered anything more than clear liquids. She may continue receiving IV fluids for up to a day after the cesarean.

The Next Few Days for the Baby

In most hospitals, babies are taken to the nursery shortly after birth for a few minutes to many hours. A few hospitals do all baby care in the mother's room, but if yours does not, you might want to accompany the baby to the nursery to watch the procedures, comfort the baby if necessary, and bring her back to her mother as soon as possible. It is rarely necessary for a baby to be separated from her mother at all, but it is more convenient for nurses and doctors to carry out routine newborn care in the nursery.

Physical Exam and Assessment

A doctor or a midwife will give the baby a thorough physical exam, checking her entire body and all her systems. It is interesting to watch the exam, which can teach you a great deal about the baby. Over the next few days you, the mother, or the staff will make certain observations of the baby: the number and quality of bowel movements, frequency of urination, frequency and length of time in feeding, respiration, temperature, pulse, and so forth. The caregiver will teach you more about these observations if they are to be your responsibility.

Bowel Movements

The baby will have a bowel movement within a few hours after birth. This bowel movement is called meconium, and it is different from later bowel movements. It is black and sticky and hard to clean. If you think of it, rub some vegetable oil all over the baby's buttocks and genitals soon after birth (before the meconium appears). It will make cleaning off the meconium easier.

Over the next few days, the baby's bowel movements will change from black to green to yellow and will become very runny. The baby may have a bowel movement almost every time she eats. This is a good sign that she is getting enough to eat.

Bathing the Baby

The baby will have a bath within the first couple of days. Unless the mother is accustomed to bathing newborns, the nurse or midwife will probably give the bath, teaching the mother at the same time. The usual advice is to give sponge baths until the dried cord falls off, but research suggests immersing a baby in water is harmless. You can probably watch or help with the bath.

Caring for the Cord

The cord stump needs to be kept clean and dry. It is cleaned with alcohol, a blue dye ("triple dye"), or water. The nurse or midwife will show you how to do this. The cord clamp is removed by the nurse or midwife, usually on the second day, leaving a black, dry stump that remains for a week or two and then drops off.

Feeding the Baby

Breastfed babies need nothing but colostrum (the first "milk" to come from the breasts) and breast milk. They do not need formula, water, or glucose water unless they have low blood sugar. It is a good idea to begin breastfeeding as soon after birth as the baby is interested. Formula-fed babies should begin receiving formula when they seem ready to suck and when their condition is stable.

For more information about your role in feeding the baby, see "Getting Started with Breastfeeding," page 215.

Circumcision

If the baby is going to be circumcised, the procedure will be done in the hospital on the second day after birth, or, in the Jewish tradition, in the home or synagogue on the eighth day. In this procedure the foreskin is surgically removed from the end of the penis, or glans. Circumcision is usually, though not always, performed without anesthesia.

Purposes of Circumcision. The surgery is done—

- To change the appearance of the penis to meet parent's preferences.
- To observe Jewish or other religious custom.
- To reduce the need for careful washing later in life.

No clear health benefits are attributable to routine circumcision of the newborn, although many physicians still advocate it for all baby boys. Some recent surveys have indicated that, although numbers are small, more uncircumcised boys may get urinary tract infections in childhood than circumcised boys. How important and how accurate this finding is, and whether circumcision is the best way to prevent these infections, remains to be investigated. Claims that AIDS and other sexually transmitted diseases may be prevented by removal of the foreskin have not been confirmed through research.

Disadvantages of Circumcision. Circumcision carries the same risks as all surgery: infection, hemorrhage, adhesions, pain, and human error.

- The procedure is clearly very painful, especially when anesthesia is not used.
- Infection or hemorrhage occurs in about one in every one hundred circumcisions. These conditions can usually be well controlled with medications and extra time in the hospital.
- There is a small possibility, especially with an inexperienced, unsupervised operator, that the surgery will be done poorly—too much or too little foreskin may be removed. Every year a few such cases make headlines.
- The circumcised penis usually takes seven to ten days to heal; during this time parents need to take special care to avoid wet diapers and other irritations to the penis, and observe it for signs of poor healing.
- If the newborn child is ill or if his penis is abnormal in structure, circumcision may be very harmful.

The popularity of this surgery is declining in the United States. The incidence of circumcision is now estimated at less than 60 percent, down from 85 percent in 1980. The cultural norm is changing, partly because of efforts by the American Academy of Pediatrics, who have stated since the early 1970s that "there is no absolute medical indication for circumcision in the neonatal (newborn) period."

Alternatives to Consider. You and the mother can—

- Leave the baby uncircumcised. If you do, learn proper care of the uncircumcised penis (see "Recommended Resources"). Teach the child proper hygiene; washing the penis is about as complex as washing the ears.

- If you decide to have the baby circumcised, request anesthesia for the procedure, and remain with the baby to comfort him.
- Leave the decision for the child to make himself when he reaches adulthood.

Baby-Care Skills

The nurse or the midwife can teach you and the mother many of the baby-care skills you need, such as—

- Bathing the baby
- Caring for the cord
- Changing the baby's diapers
- Positioning the baby for feeding
- Feeding the baby (techniques)
- Burping the baby
- Soothing a fussy baby
- Caring for the baby's genitals

These skills are easily learned, but you may feel more confident about handling the baby if you get some instruction.

The Next Few Days for the Mother

For the mother, the early postpartum period is marked by fatigue, emotional highs and lows, preoccupation with the baby, some pain, and an array of physical changes that affect most parts of her body.

She may be tired and excited at the same time, finding it difficult to sleep, but unable to exert herself very much without feeling worn out. A shower or a short walk is enough to send her straight back to bed.

The mother may be surprised by the variety of physical changes she experiences; these physical changes will require more attention than she ever expected.

The Uterus

As described earlier (page 196), the nurse or midwife and the mother herself should check the uterus frequently to be sure it remains contracted. Remind her to do this.

Afterpains

Especially if she has had a child before, the mother will feel afterpains, which can be quite painful, when the baby suckles or when the uterus contracts. Remind her to use her relaxation and breathing techniques. Pain medications are available if afterpains are severe. Afterpains go away in a few days.

Vaginal Discharge

The mother will have a vaginal discharge, called lochia, which is similar to a menstrual period. It starts out as a heavy red flow containing some clots, and gradually diminishes; it lasts from two to six weeks. If the lochia suddenly increases or if the mother passes large, golf-ball-size clots, call her caregiver, because it may mean that she is bleeding from a blood vessel at the former site of the placenta.

The Perineum

After a vaginal birth, the mother's perineum will be sore, especially if she has had stitches. In any case, she may have swelling and bruising. You can suggest the following comfort measures:

- Applying an ice pack helps, especially during the first twenty-four hours.
- Sitting in a bath of warm water (a sitz bath) for twenty minutes, two or three times a day, is soothing. She should not wash in this water; it should be kept clean.
- Carefully patting her perineum dry or squirting warm water from a bottle after urinating or having a bowel movement is less irritating than wiping with toilet paper.
- Applying witch hazel–soaked pads to stitches and hemorrhoids is soothing.
- Doing the pelvic floor contraction (Kegel) exercise promotes healing, reduces swelling, and restores strength: the mother tightens the muscles around her vagina and urethra as she would if she were trying to hold back urine (see page 15). If it is done fifty to one hundred times a day, this exercise can also help to restore muscle tone in the area that was stretched during birth.

Elimination

You may be surprised at how preoccupied the mother becomes with bowel movements and urination. These functions are more difficult than usual because her perineum is sore, her abdominal muscles are temporarily weak, her food and fluid intake have been interrupted by labor, and, now that it is no longer crowded by the baby, her bladder has an increased capacity.

If she is unable to urinate, even with all the tricks (running a faucet, urinating in the bath or shower, and so forth), she may have to have a catheter placed in her bladder to empty it. This is unpleasant, but it is better than letting her bladder become distended.

To help the mother avoid or reduce difficulties with the first bowel movement after giving birth, remind her to eat and drink high-fiber foods: prune juice, other juices, raw fruits and vegetables, bran breads or cereals, and so forth. Bulk-producing laxatives may also help.

Pain Following Cesarean Delivery

Post-cesarean pain results from the incision, from the stitches or clamps closing it, and from gas that commonly builds up in the mother's abdomen after this surgery. Activities such as turning over, getting out of bed, walking, and nursing the baby are usually very painful for a few days, but they hasten recovery. Help as much as you can to make these activities easier for her, by giving her a hand as she gets out of bed, offering a supportive arm as she walks, providing a pillow for her lap as she nurses the baby. The mother will gradually begin feeling better each day.

Clamps or stitches are removed on the second or third day after the delivery. The procedure is not very painful, and the pain from the incision will then decrease.

To help her reduce abdominal pain, encourage the mother to do the following:

- When rolling from her back to her side, she should first bend her knees so that her feet are flat on the bed; then she should raise her hips, twist them to one side, and roll her shoulders to the side. This is much easier and far less painful than rolling over the usual way.
- She should avoid gas-producing foods (lentils and beans, foods in the cabbage family, cold or carbonated beverages).
- Before getting out of bed the first few times, she should warm up by doing an ankle-circling exercise and by raising her arms above her head several times.
- When holding the baby on her lap, she should place a pillow over the incision to protect it.
- She should ask the nurse to show her other ways to hold the baby to avoid pressure on her incision.

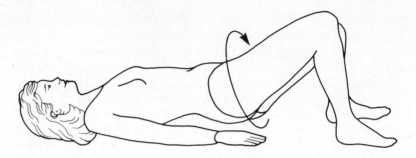

To reduce pain when rolling from her back to her side, the mother who has had a cesarean should raise and twist her hips before turning her shoulders.

Discharge from the Hospital

The mother has some choice regarding when she will leave the hospital, especially when her and the baby's postpartum course are going smoothly. She should plan in advance and consider these factors when deciding:

- *Cost.* Hospital costs are very high. If she leaves the hospital early, she can save money.
- *The hospital environment.* Some hospitals provide a restful, quiet environment with kind, helpful, and competent nurses, good food, and comfortable rooms. Others offer just the opposite.
- *Benefits of staying.* If she stays longer, will she be taught more about baby care and feeding? Will she feel more secure in the hospital than at home?
- *Contact with loved ones.* Some hospitals restrict visiting hours or do not allow older children to visit their mothers. Others place few restrictions on visitors.
- *The situation at home.* Can she rest at home? Will she have help with meals, housework, care of the baby, and other children? From whom? You, relatives or friends, a hired helper, a nurse?
- *Mother's and baby's health.* A short hospital stay is a possibility only if the mother and baby are doing well. They are both examined before leaving.

Many hospitals have early discharge programs. Mothers leave as early as six hours after a normal vaginal birth, or three days after a cesarean. The hospitals provide phone follow-up and one or two home visits by a nurse within the first few days. Mothers and their partners are taught which observations to make of mother and baby and are given guidelines on when to call the caregiver (mother's or baby's). With good instruction of the parents, follow-up care, and help for the mother at home, early discharge programs are safe and popular. Without these features, a serious problem (such as poor nursing, jaundice, infection, or excessive bleeding) could go unnoticed for too long, causing unnecessary risks to the mother and the baby.

Homecoming

Before the mother and the baby come home, take a moment to think about what they are coming home to. Is the house a mess? Is the sink full of dishes? Is the bed unmade? Is the baby's place (basket, box, crib, changing area) ready? There is nothing more disheartening for the mother than returning home to chaos. You want her to feel glad to get home, so try to provide a pleasant homecoming.

Prepare the home:

- Make the bed with fresh linens.
- Tidy up the house, do the dishes, and so forth.
- Make sure good food is available.
- Have a stack of fresh diapers ready (call a diaper service or buy some).
- Have a few welcoming touches around the house—fresh flowers, a "Welcome Home" poster.

Prepare for the ride home:

- Install the infant car seat.
- Tidy up the inside of the car.
- Have enough gas that you don't have to stop on the way home.
- Make sure the mother and the baby have clothes to wear home and that the baby has a blanket or two.
- Ask visitors not to come until at least the next day.

When the mother and the baby arrive home, you may all feel like celebrating. And with good reason! When you bring the baby home, you're introducing him to his own new world. The mother, too, may feel she has been away a long time and may be relieved to be in familiar surroundings once again. She has been through a lot and, unfortunately, fatigue will set in very soon. Perhaps the best thing for her to do is get into bed, snuggle with her loved ones, bask in the warm feelings.

After a Home Birth

If the baby was born at home, there is probably a big clean-up operation ahead—dishes, lots of laundry, lots of trash, a bed to make with fresh linens. Sometimes everyone leaves soon after the birth, wanting to give the new family some quiet time together. And you are left with a huge clean-up project. Plan in advance, so you can avoid this situation:

- Ask the caregiver about cleanup ahead of time: (1) How much does she or he do? (2) What will need to be done? (3) What happens to the placenta? Sometimes the caregiver takes it and disposes of it. Some families bury it and plant a tree or a bush over it.
- Have large trash bags available during labor—one for disposable trash, one for laundry. As items are used, they can go right into the appropriate bags.
- If there are extra people available, assign ongoing and after-birth clean-up tasks: picking up and washing dishes; putting food away; doing laundry; taking trash out; straightening up the house.

The Mother's Postpartum Emotions

During the early postpartum period the mother's emotions are changeable and unpredictable. One moment she may be rapturous and full of energy; the next, tired, frustrated, and in tears. Her body's sudden physiological changes, in hormone production and body function—as she goes from supporting the growth of a fetus during pregnancy to expelling a baby to resuming a nonpregnant state—take an emotional toll. Add to that her inevitable fatigue from loss of sleep during labor and during the first few days after the birth, as well as the stress of a profound role change, and it is not surprising that she is volatile.

If you are the mother's life partner as well as her birth partner, you have your own share of emotional adjustments—the role change to parenthood, your own fatigue, and a complete disruption in lifestyle. Even if you are a relative or a friend helping out temporarily, you are probably tired from the birth experience and from the strain of caring for the mother and the new baby.

As two tired people with a great many needs, you will be sustained through this stressful time by your underlying feelings for each other and by the joy and commitment you share in having a new baby. It helps to know that this situation *will* get better. Following are some suggestions for getting through the emotional ups and downs of the first few days after the baby is born.

Postpartum Blues

If the mother seems sad or cries a lot (we call this postpartum blues) you may be surprised if this is not her usual style; you may feel helpless or guilty, believing that you are to blame or that it is up to you to make it right; you may worry about her; you may feel angry with her; or you may wonder if this situation is going to be permanent.

What Can You Do about Postpartum Blues? Here are some suggestions:

- First of all, let the mother cry. She does not have to have a reason. She needs to be able to cry without you (and everyone else) feeling you must help her get over it. Accept her need to cry, with patience, tenderness, and empathy.
- Do not blame yourself. You almost certainly did not do anything to make her cry.
- Know that almost every woman sheds tears and goes on an emotional roller coaster for a few days; emotions are close to the surface after childbirth.
- Realize that this will probably pass after a few days. Give her time. Encourage her to nap and to rest.
- Ask her friends and relatives, especially those who have had children, to visit.
- Feel free to call the mother's caregiver, childbirth educator, or breastfeeding counselor if you are worried about her.
- Look into mothers' groups or postpartum classes. They are becoming very popular as places where these feelings can be shared openly and discussed.

On rare occasions these blue feelings predominate and last for weeks. If you think this is happening, or if you feel under undue pressure, the mother may have a postpartum depression. Discuss your concerns with the mother and call the resource people already mentioned. Sometimes a referral to a social worker, psychologist, or psychiatrist for counseling or therapy is appropriate and very helpful. Sometimes a complete physical exam, with blood tests to check levels of various hormones, reveals a physical condition that could be contributing to depression. Sometimes a support group alone can help a mother recover from her depressed feelings. Consider these options if the mother is predominantly depressed after a few weeks.

Practical Matters at Home

Much of the turmoil of the postpartum period can be avoided if you're prepared for it in advance and if you can simplify your lives for a while. Whether you are the mother's life partner or a relative or friend helping out, the following suggestions will help all of you get through these first days until the household becomes more settled.

Fatigue

The mother is tired. You may be tired, too. If you were her birth partner and are now her "at home" support person, you are probably running out of energy yourself. Fatigue makes *everything* worse. Until things have settled into a comfortable routine, give a high priority to getting enough sleep. It will not all come in one stretch at night; everyone will have to nap. How much sleep does each member of the household need in order to function well? Make it a goal to get that much sleep each day. Nap with the baby on your chest. Take turns napping. Unplug the phone and put a "Do Not Disturb" sign on the front door during nap times.

Fussy, Crying Baby

Entire books have been written about fussy babies (see "Recommended Resources"). In the first few days, a fussy baby can usually be soothed by—

- Feeding or burping.
- Changing her diaper.
- Letting the baby suck on your (clean) little finger: place your finger in her mouth with the nail down on her tongue and the soft pad touching the roof of her mouth; she might take it more eagerly at first if you wet it.
- Swaddling the baby snugly in a blanket.
- Picking her up, rocking or walking her, or changing her position in bed. "Wear" the baby by carrying her close to your body in a baby carrier or sling.
- Creating "white noise"—the sounds of a dishwasher or a washing machine; peaceful recorded music; or, best of all, lullabies crooned in the baby's ear.

Don't leave a tiny baby crying. The first few days after birth are a major adjustment for the baby, too. A newborn needs the comfort and security of feeling your bodies and hearing your voices nearby. Do not worry about spoiling the baby: you cannot spoil her by meeting her basic needs.

Scheduling the Baby's Sleeping and Feeding

Don't even try to get the baby on a schedule in the first few weeks. Instead, discover the baby's own "schedule" and pattern your life around that. Focus on meeting the baby's needs; try to figure out how he tells you he is hungry, curious, interested, bored, uncomfortable, or overstimulated. Let the baby call the shots. It is much easier for the household to adjust to the baby at first than to make the baby adjust to the household. Make it your goal to meet the baby's needs, as expressed by the baby—you will all be happier if you do. Read *The Amazing Newborn* (see "Recommended Resources") to help you understand the baby.

Meals

Time for meal preparation hardly exists during the busy first days at home; yet good food, quickly available, is a must. Try the following:

- *Prepare meals in advance.* Before the birth, prepare a few dishes—such as soups, casseroles, and stews—that will either keep for several days or will freeze.
- *Purchase quick, nutritious, tasty foods.* Foods that need little or no preparation—that you can grab and eat—are good choices for the first few weeks. These foods include yogurt, fruit, granola and nuts, cottage cheese, hard cheese, raw vegetables, and whole-grain breads and crackers. Try to have these on hand before the birth so you won't have to go shopping right away.
- *Fix dishes that last for a while.* For example, you can roast a turkey and pick from it for a week; or wash, cut, and chill raw vegetables to keep in the refrigerator for munching.
- *Accept food from friends and relatives.* If people ask how they can help, tell them you'd love a main dish.
- *Remember the mother's dietary needs.* Her postpartum diet should be as good as her pregnancy diet was. If she is breastfeeding she will need two or three hundred calories more than normal each day. She will also need two quarts or more of liquids each day.

Household Chores

The first few days at home are busy and full of adjustments. Do the mother and yourself a big favor: plan to do the minimum in the way of household chores—just enough to maintain sanity. It may be easier if you have "supercleaned" before the baby was born; if you haven't, just close your eyes and let things accumulate for a while. Simplify your lives so you are free to care for and enjoy the baby and to get enough rest.

11
Getting Started with Breastfeeding

*Y*our role when the mother breastfeeds may seem unclear, because it is not as simple as taking over the feeding for her when she is tired. It is more a matter of supporting her decision to breastfeed and helping simplify her life while she does it. It really helps if you have some knowledge and conviction about the advantages of breastfeeding.

Advantages of Breastfeeding

The advantages of breastfeeding are many, for everyone involved. For the family—

- It costs much less to breastfeed than to formula-feed.
- Formula preparation and bottle washing chores are avoided.

For the mother—

- Breastfeeding hastens her uterus' return to normal by causing it to contract with every feeding.
- Hormones associated with breastfeeding cause relaxation and feelings of contentment.
- Once the initial learning period has passed, most women find breastfeeding very satisfying.

For the baby—

- Breast milk is perfectly suited to the baby's nutritional requirements.
- Breast milk contains substances (immunoglobulins and antibodies from the mother) that provide important protection against illness.
- Breast milk changes in composition as the baby grows and his nutritional requirements change.
- Problems with allergies, indigestion, and overfeeding are fewer with breast milk than with formula.
- The milk is always at the right temperature and instantly available.
- Long-term advantages of superior jaw development, reduced likelihood of obesity, and better ability to handle dietary fats are also attributed to breastfeeding.

Because of all these advantages, most mothers today decide to breastfeed. There are challenges to overcome, however, before breastfeeding becomes easy, quick, and convenient. A lack of experience may lead parents to doubt whether the baby is getting enough milk, to worry that the baby nurses too often or not enough. They may not feel they can trust the process. There are several ways to alleviate these doubts: take a breastfeeding class or a parenting class; read a good book (see "Recommended Resources"); check with women who have breastfed or with a breastfeeding counselor; be sure the baby's doctor is supportive and knowledgeable about breastfeeding. The following information can help you get the breastfeeding relationship off to a good start.

Getting Off to a Good Start

A good start with breastfeeding depends on—

- Frequent feeding of the baby on demand (whenever the baby fusses), beginning as soon after birth as the baby will suckle.
- A good "latch" between the baby's mouth and the breast.
- Availability of advice from a knowledgeable person.
- *Your* help and positive support.
- Freedom from excessive difficulty. I mention this because, on rare occasions, a woman who wants very much to breastfeed has one problem after another, even when working closely with a breastfeeding counselor. If she finally gives up in exasperation and disappointment, she may feel depressed, uncertain, and ashamed over her decision. If breastfeeding is the way most of her friends and family choose to feed their babies, a woman may feel a great deal

of pressure to do the same. But only she can balance the advantages and disadvantages of her situation. She should get the best support and advice available, and if feeding problems are still insurmountable, she is right to formula-feed. And she should be forgiving of herself. Your understanding and support of her decision will help her immensely.

Early Concerns

Breastfeeding does not come easily at first to most women. It takes two to four weeks to reach the point where all the mother has to do is put the baby near her breast to get him to latch on and suckle. In the meantime, problems such as temporary nipple soreness, lack of sleep, and concern over milk supply have to be overcome. Both you and the mother need information and guidelines on what is normal and how to solve these problems.

Milk Supply

How can you know if the mother is making enough milk? If the baby needs to nurse frequently, does it mean the mother is not making enough milk to satisfy the baby's hunger? It sometimes is difficult to trust such an imprecise process as breastfeeding. These facts may help:

- The mother makes a very small quantity of colostrum for the first two to four days after birth. It is enough to satisfy all the baby's nutritional requirements for the first few days.
- After a few days, the colostrum is replaced by milk. The frequency and total amount of time spent suckling help determine when the milk "comes in" and how much milk the mother makes.
- Young babies normally nurse often—eight to eighteen times a day. This may come as a surprise to the mother, who will spend many hours every day breastfeeding. Generally, the more a baby suckles, the more milk the mother makes.
- Babies do not nurse at regular intervals; they "bunch up" several feedings in a row, and then go without feeding for a relatively long stretch. It is not unusual for a baby to nurse four times in six hours, then sleep for three or four hours before the next feeding.
- Adequacy of breast milk can be determined by these signs: how the breasts feel (more heavy and full before a feeding than afterward); whether milk can be expressed from the breasts; whether the baby is wetting her diapers and having bowel movements (after

the milk comes in, six to eight wet diapers a day and a bowel movement at almost every feeding are good signs for the first four weeks); and whether the baby noticeably swallows after every few sucks. Weight gain is a clear sign that the baby is getting enough milk, although the baby may not begin to gain until he is a few days old.

If the baby appears not to be getting enough milk, try the Twenty-four-hour Cure (page 220).

Fatigue and Lack of Sleep in the Mother

Because young babies nurse frequently and sometimes fuss during the night, long stretches of sleep are no longer possible for the mother, or for you if you're trying to help at night. Sleep tends to come in the form of two- or three-hour naps between feedings. This normal change in sleep patterns is not a major problem if you and the mother can catch up with a nap or two during the day. If not, fatigue sets in, and it interferes with all aspects of parenting and daily living.

The mother may get more sleep, and the baby may fuss less, if she nurses him in bed at night and naps or sleeps with or near him. This way she can doze as she feeds the baby and does not have to get up as much. But if the mother is uncomfortable having the baby in bed with her, this solution will not work. If fatigue becomes a major concern for the mother, try the Twenty-four-hour Cure (page 220).

Breast Pain

Breast pain in the first few days may be caused by—

- *Engorgement.* Breast milk replaces colostrum after one and a half to four days. It usually "comes in" over a period of eight to twelve hours. Some women's breasts become extremely full and painful, or engorged, making it difficult for the baby to latch on. The solution is to empty the breasts by nursing the baby. If the breasts are too firm to allow the baby to get a good latch, the mother should soften them as follows: She should express a small amount of milk before she feeds the baby, either by hand or with a mechanical pump. She can apply hot packs or let the shower run over her breasts to start the flow of milk. Engorgement subsides after a few days, when a balance is reached between the amount of milk needed by the baby and the amount produced by the mother.

Engorgement sometimes occurs even in women who do not breastfeed, but with lack of suckling and medications to stop milk production, it passes.

- *Prolonged, vigorous suckling.* Some babies suck harder and longer than others. Early nipple soreness may be greater with such babies, but it passes within a week or so if the latch (the connection between mouth and breast) is good. Trying to limit the baby's suckling time to three or five minutes does not reduce soreness and is unnecessary. If the baby's suckling is very prolonged, however, the mother could try switching breasts after ten or twelve minutes.

  It is important not to fall into the trap of giving a bottle to "rest" the breasts, unless the soreness is extreme. Some nipple soreness is to be expected at first. It is considered within normal limits if soreness occurs each time the baby latches but then subsides after about a minute of suckling, and the rest of the feeding is comfortable. This type of soreness lasts only a few days to a week.

- *Thrush.* A yeast infection in the baby's mouth can spread to the mother's nipples, causing deep, severe pain during nursing. If the mother has this kind of pain, check the baby's mouth for patches of white film on his gums, his tongue, or the roof of his mouth. Check the mother's nipples as well for irritated or whitish patches. Call the baby's doctor if you suspect thrush.

- *A poor latch.* Improper suckling may cause the mother excessive nipple soreness. If the baby nibbles or "clicks" (breaks the suction with each suck), the mother's nipples will hurt more than is normally expected. Her nurse or midwife, a breastfeeding counselor, her childbirth educator, or a good book on breastfeeding (see "Recommended Resources") can help with the latch.

  A good latch means the baby is positioned correctly and her mouth is wide open to take in a large amount of *areola* (the dark circle around the nipple). When being held in the mother's arms, the baby should be on her side ("tummy to tummy") rather than on her back. Other good positions are lying side by side and the "football" or "clutch" hold, in which the mother sits up, holding the baby beside and facing her. The baby's feet are behind the mother, and the baby's head is held by the mother at her breast. In all positions, pillows are useful to prop the mother and the baby comfortably. In all positions, too, the baby's face is held very close to the breast, so she doesn't pull hard on the nipple with every suckle. If soreness persists throughout a feeding, it may be because of a poor latch. This should definitely be checked.

Treating Sore Nipples. The mother can treat nipple soreness in the following ways:

- Rub a little colostrum or milk into the nipples and allow them to dry.
- Dry the nipples after each feeding with a hair dryer (on its lowest setting) held at arm's length. This feels wonderful, and thoroughly dries the nipples.
- Apply ice to the nipples just before a feeding to reduce sensation.
- Soak black (not herbal) tea bags in warm water and place them on the nipples for about ten minutes two or three times a day. Tea contains a small amount of tannic acid, which seems to toughen skin.
- Rub unscented hydrous lanolin into the nipples (unless she is allergic to wool).
- Avoid washing the nipples with soap, even if they are protected by a coating of lanolin. Soap makes soreness worse. Rinsing with water is sufficient for cleanliness.
- Expose the breasts to the air by lowering the flaps of her bra, or by wearing no bra.
- Begin each nursing on the less sore side.
- Reduce suckling time to ten or twelve minutes per side until the soreness begins to subside. If soreness is extreme and her nipples are bleeding, the mother may need to stop breastfeeding and pump milk for a day or so to get healing started. During this time, give the baby pumped breast milk or formula from a bottle.
- Take acetaminophen, not aspirin or ibuprofen, if she needs pain medications.
- Consult a breastfeeding counselor, childbirth educator, physician, or a good book (see "Recommended Resources").

The Twenty-four-hour Cure

During the first few weeks after birth, the mother and baby are perfecting the art of breastfeeding. The Twenty-four-hour Cure can solve some of the problems that arise, such as the following:

- Doubts about whether the mother is making enough milk.
- Fatigue, lack of sleep, or anxiety in the mother.
- Lack of appetite, poor nourishment, or low fluid intake in the mother.
- Slow weight gain or weight loss in the baby.

- "Nipple confusion"—that is, the baby seems to prefer a rubber nipple or nipple shield to the mother's breast.

The cure has two purposes:

1. To nurture the mother, by giving her complete rest, plenty of good food and drink, and freedom from all responsibility other than feeding and fondling her baby.
2. To nurture the baby, by encouraging prolonged skin-to-skin contact with the mother and constant access to her breast.

Here is how to do the cure:

- Set aside a full twenty-four hours when the mother can have your help. Use your day off, or get a loved one or friend to take your place. Twenty-four hours with help is essential.
- Make sure the mother does not have sore, blistered, or cracked nipples when she begins the cure. The causes of the soreness need to be addressed before starting the cure (see "Treating Sore Nipples," page 220).
- The mother goes to bed with the baby. They both wear as little clothing as possible under the bedcovers so the baby can get lots of warm skin-to-skin contact, which will heighten his suckling reflex and interest in feeding.
- The mother may read, watch TV, chat with you (no visitors, please), or, most important, doze. The extra sleep makes a big difference, even though it comes in short snatches.
- She gets out of bed *only to go to the bathroom*—not to eat, answer the phone, do housework, or anything else.
- Supply her with liquids; place water or juice within her reach. She should drink about two quarts of liquid during the twenty-four hours.
- Fix tasty, nutritious meals for her. Tempt her appetite with foods she is unlikely to prepare for herself. If she has been relying on take-out fast foods or cold ready-to-eat foods, she will love a hot, home-cooked meal or two.
- The baby should stay in bed with her, except when a diaper change is necessary, or when the baby is fussy (but not willing to nurse) and needs to be walked or rocked. Then you should take care of the baby.
- Whenever the baby awakens or seems at all interested in suckling, the mother offers her breast. The whole purpose is to get the baby to suckle as much as possible. Do not give the baby a bottle of

either formula or breast milk, unless he is seriously underweight. In that case, you need to consult the baby's doctor, a breastfeeding consultant, or a breastfeeding support organization, such as La Leche League (listed in the white pages of the phone book).

The combination of rest and nourishment for the mother and skin-to-skin contact and unlimited suckling for the baby almost always results in a marked increase in the mother's milk production and improved suckling by the baby.

If the mother is unable to stick closely to this plan, or if the Twenty-four-hour Cure fails to solve the problem, consult the baby's doctor, a breastfeeding consultant, or La Leche League.

When to Give the Baby a Bottle

You may be looking forward to feeding the baby from a bottle, but it is wise not to rush bottle feeding with a breastfed baby, for two reasons:

1. While the baby is getting used to the human nipple, it may be confusing for him to suck from a rubber nipple. Different sucking techniques—different mouth and jaw motions—are required for human and rubber nipples.

2. When he takes milk from a bottle the baby spends less time suckling at the breast. This may slow milk production, because it is the suckling that stimulates the breasts to produce. A shortage of breast milk may result.

If you want to feed the baby with a bottle, wait a few weeks, until the baby easily latches on and suckles at the breast and until the milk supply is clearly plentiful. The mother can then express her own milk for you to feed, or you can feed formula from the bottle. Help with burping, bathing, soothing, and diapering the baby in the meantime.

Although most babies take the bottle quite easily, some are reluctant to take it after becoming accustomed to the breast. Allow a couple of weeks for the baby to learn to use the bottle before the mother leaves him for a significant length of time with you or a babysitter. It is usually preferable that someone other than the mother gives the bottle to the baby; he may insist on the mother's breast if she is right there. With persistence on your part, the baby will eventually take the bottle. If it seems too difficult to get the baby to take it, you can squirt milk into a corner of his mouth with an eyedropper.

Once Breastfeeding Is Established

By two to six weeks of age, most babies and their mothers find breastfeeding to be a pleasant, quick, convenient method of feeding. Although there may still be some hurdles ahead, the greatest difficulties are behind most breastfeeding mothers and babies by this time, and the closeness and pleasure they share are most satisfying.

Parting Words

The family is launched. The baby is born and getting used to the world; the mother is no longer pregnant and is adjusting to being on constant call. Your job as birth partner is over. The excitement is over and you may feel strangely let down.

Now what? It will take a while to absorb and integrate all that has happened. This birth has transformed you into a parent, or grandparent, or more-special-than-ever friend. You will never be the same, and you will always treasure this experience.

Congratulations.

RECOMMENDED RESOURCES

Following is a list of books and pamphlets that provide further discussion of pregnancy, birth, and parenting. Lynn Moen, president of the Birth and Life Bookstore, helped me to select the books on the list and provided the descriptions that accompany them. The books are available from these sources:

Birth and Life Bookstore
PO Box 70625
Seattle, Washington 98107-0625

ICEA Bookcenter
PO Box 20048
Minneapolis, Minnesota 55420

Childbirth Preparation

Anderson, Sandra Van Dam, and Simkin, Penny. *Birth—Through Children's Eyes*, 1981. Complete guide for professionals and parents about children at birth. Pennypress.

Baldwin, Rahima. *Special Delivery: The Complete Guide to Informed Birth*, rev. 1986. Practical guide for couples who want to take greater responsibility for the birth of their babies, with sections about hospital options, preventing cesareans, and emotional aspects of childbirth. (Les Femmes) Celest.

Jones, Carl. *Sharing Birth: Father's Guide to Giving Support during Labor*, 1985. Clear, well-written guide showing what a man can do to alleviate the pain and fear of the mother's labor, and to share the joy of birth. Quill/William Morrow.

Jones, Carl. *Mind over Labor: Using the Mind's Power to Reduce the Pain in Childbirth*, 1987. Eight-step method of using mental imagery to prepare for a safe, happy birth. Viking Penguin.

Kitzinger, Sheila. *The Complete Book of Pregnancy and Childbirth*, 1980. Comprehensive, splendidly illustrated guide and reference by an international expert. Alfred A. Knopf.

Kitzinger, Sheila. *Your Baby, Your Way: Making Pregnancy Decisions and Birth Plans*, 1987. Supportive guide to help women choose among the alternatives in pregnancy and childbirth. Pantheon/Random House.

Lansky, Vicki, and eds. *Consumer Guide. Complete Pregnancy and Baby Book*, 1987. Illustrated, encyclopedic guide from conception through the toddler years. Publications International.

Lieberman, Adrienne. *Easing Labor Pain: The Complete Guide for Achieving a More Comfortable Birth*, 1987. Causes of childbirth pain and all resources to deal with it. Doubleday.

Ohashi, Wataru, and Hoover, Mary. *Natural Childbirth, the Eastern Way: A Healthy Pregnancy and Delivery Through Shiatsu*, 1983. Techniques and exercises to use alone or in conjunction with other childbirth methods to prepare for childbirth. Ballantine Books.

Robertson, Patricia Anne, and Berlin, Peggy Henning. *The Premature Labor Handbook: Successfully Sustaining Your High-Risk Pregnancy*, 1986. Preventing prematurity to ensure baby's maximal health. Doubleday.

Rosegg, Susan McCutcheon. *Natural Childbirth, the Bradley Way*, 1985. Well-illustrated manual on "husband-coached" birth. Dutton.

Savage, Beverly, and Simkin, Diana. *Preparation for Birth: The Complete Guide to the Lamaze Method*, 1987. Outlines options for choosing doctors, medications, hospital or home delivery; from pregnancy to post partum. Ballantine/Random House.

Simkin, Penny; Whalley, Janet; and Keppler, Ann. *Pregnancy, Childbirth, and the Newborn: A Complete Guide for Expectant Parents*, 1984. Thorough, well-illustrated, up-to-date guide; provides a broad framework for parents to develop their own way of giving birth. Meadowbrook.

Cesarean Birth

Ancheta, Ruth. *VBAC Source Book: Vaginal Birth after Cesarean*, 1987. Summarizes studies on VBACs for professionals and parents. Birth Information.

Donovan, Bonnie. *The Cesarean Birth Experience*, rev. 1985. Practical, comprehensive, and reassuring guide to family-centered cesarean birth. Beacon Press.

Pamphlets

Better Babies Series. Growing list of low-cost pamphlets by experts on topics of interest to expectant and new parents; four or eight pages each. Pennypress.

Anderson, Sandra Van Dam, and del Guidice, Georgeanne. *Siblings, Birth and the Newborn*, 1983.

Edwards, Margot. *Childbirth: A Teenager's Guide*, 1979.

Edwards, Margot. *A Working Mother Can Breastfeed When . . .* , 1983.

Edwards, Margot, and Simkin, Penny. *Obstetric Tests and Technology: A Consumer's Guide*, 1984.

Edwards, Margot. *When Food Is Love*, 1988.

Gruen, Dawn. *Babies and Jobs: Concerns and Choices*, 1986.

Gruen, Dawn. *The New Parent: A Spectrum of Postpartum Adjustment*, 1988.

Hoffman, Susan Greene. *Bedrest in Pregnancy*, 1985.

Jones, Carl; Goer, Henci; and Simkin, Penny. *The Labor Support Guide: For Fathers, Family and Friends*, 1984.

Keolker, Kathy. *Cesarean Birth: A Special Delivery*, 1983.

Kitzinger, Sheila. *Sex During Pregnancy*, 1979.

Kitzinger, Sheila. *Sex after the Baby Comes*, 1980.

Myrabo, Jessica. *The First Days after Birth: Care of Mother and Baby*, 1983.

Reinke, Carla. *Herpes in Pregnancy*, 1982.

Simkin, Penny, and Edwards, Margot. *When Your Baby Has Jaundice*, 1979.

Simkin, Penny, and Reinke, Carla. *Planning Your Baby's Birth*, 1980.

Wallerstein, Edward. *When Your Baby Boy Is Not Circumcised*, 1982.

Wallerstein, Edward. *The Circumcision Decision*, 1987.

Weston, Marianne Brorup; Simkin, Penny; and Keolker, Kathy. *Vaginal Birth after Cesarean*, 1987.

White, Rulena. *Fitness in Pregnancy*, 1984.

Pregnancy Loss

Borg, Susan, and Lasker, Judith. *When Pregnancy Fails*, 1986. For families coping with miscarriage, stillbirth, and infant death, and their support networks. Beacon Press.

Schwieber, Pat, and Kirk, Paul. *When Hello Means Goodbye*, rev. 1985. Sensitive booklet for parents whose child dies at birth or shortly afterward. University of Oregon Health Science Center.

Premature Baby

Harrison, Helen. *The Premature Baby Book: A Parent's Guide to Coping and Caring in the First Years*, 1984. Comprehensive, well-illustrated guide to the emotional, medical, and practical issues following the birth of a premature baby. St. Martin's Press.

Lieberman, Adrienne. *The Premie Parents' Handbook: A Lifeline for the New Parents of a Premature Baby*, 1984. Comforting, easy-to-use guide on neonatal care and premie development. Meadowbrook.

Breastfeeding

Dana, Nancy, and Price, Anne. *Working Woman's Guide to Breastfeeding*, rev. 1987. Addresses the special needs of mothers who work outside their homes. Meadowbrook.

Huggins, Kathleen. *The Nursing Mother's Companion*, 1986. Lucid, troubleshooting aid for the new mother learning how to nurse. Harvard Common Press.

Fathering

Greenberg, Martin. *The Birth of a Father*, 1985. Gentle directives for the new father, to help him become "engrossed" and involved in his baby's care. Continuum/Scribner.

Kort, Carol, and Friedland, Ronnie. *The Fathers' Book: Shared Experiences*, 1986. Seventy fathers speak out about what it really means to be a father today. G. K. Hall.

Sears, William. *Becoming a Father*, 1986. The joys and problems of parenthood from the male perspective. La Leche League.

Shapiro, Jerrold Lee. *When Men Are Pregnant: Needs and Concerns of Expectant Fathers*, 1987. To help expectant fathers make better sense of the experiences of the earliest days of fatherhood. Impact.

Snydal, Larry, and Jones, Carl. *The New Father Survival Guide*, 1987. Light-hearted and sympathetic aid to coping with early fatherhood. Franklin Watts.

Sullivan, S. Adams. *The Father's Almanac*, 1980. Practical advice and ideas for men who enjoy the fun and challenge of raising young children. Doubleday.

For Children

Kitzinger, Sheila, and Nilsson, Lennart. *Being Born*, 1986. Poetic text and magnificent photos made this book about conception and birth an instant classic. Grossett and Dunlap.

Malecki, Maryann. *Mom and Dad and I Are Having a Baby*, 1980. Picture book to prepare children three to seven years old to be present at a birth. Pennypress.

Malecki, Maryann. *Our Brand New Baby*, rev. 1985. Introduces a three- to seven-year-old child to the joys and frustrations of a new baby in the family. Pennypress.

Twins

Alexander, Terry Pink. *Make Room for Twins*, 1987. An insightful guide to twin pregnancy, delivery, and parenting. Bantam Books.

Gromada, Karen Kerkhoff. *Mothering Multiples*, rev. 1985. Practical guide for parents, particularly breastfeeding mothers, of twins. La Leche League.

Leigh, Gillian. *All about Twins: A Handbook for Parents*, 1984. Practical guidelines by a physician and mother of twins. Routledge and Kegan Paul.

Parenting

Galinsky, Ellen. *The Six Stages of Parenthood*, repr. 1987. How parents change and grow in reactions to the demands of parenting their developing children. Addison-Wesley.

Leach, Penelope. *Your Baby and Child: From Birth to Age Five*, 1978. Comprehensive, sensitive guide to child care and development; beautifully illustrated. Alfred A. Knopf.

Spock, Benjamin. *Dr. Spock's Baby and Child Care*, rev. 1985. The revised classic source book for parents. Dutton.

Working and Childcare

Brazelton, T. Berry. *Working and Caring*, 1985. How working parents can juggle work and parenting. Addison-Wesley.

Maynard, Fredelle. *The Child Care Crisis: The Thinking Parent's Guide to Day Care*, 1986. Helps parents make wise decisions about the care of their young children. Penguin.

Yeiser, Lin. *Nannies, Au Pairs and Mother's Helpers*, 1987. A thorough guide to alternatives in home child care. Vintage/Random House.

Infant Development

Brazelton, T. Berry. *Infants and Mothers: Differences in Development*, rev. 1983. Variations in normal first-year development in three "typical" infants; includes single and working mothers. Dell.

Klaus, Marshall and Phyllis. *The Amazing Newborn: Discovering and Enjoying Your Baby's Natural Abilities*, 1985. Discusses the development of baby's sensory perception during the first few weeks and months of life. Addison-Wesley.

Leach, Penelope. *The First Six Months: Getting Together with Your Baby*, 1987. Making the most of a baby's first six months. Alfred Knopf/Borzoi.

Sears, William. *Growing Together: A Parent's Guide to Baby's First Year*, 1987. To help you know and grow with your baby. Includes over two hundred black and white and color photos. La Leche League.

Thoman, Evelyn. *Born Dancing*, 1987. How intuitive parents understand their baby's unspoken language and natural rhythms. Harper and Row.

Audio Tapes

Hart, Mickey. *Music to Be Born By*, 1989. Produced by the percussionist for the Grateful Dead, this tape features his son's fetal heartbeat. The rhythmic patterns comfort mother and child through labor, and before and after as well. Rykodisc RCD 20112/RACS.

Simkin, Penny. *Relax for Childbirth*, 1988. A sixteen-minute relaxation exercise with a soothing narration that includes positive visualization and music. Pennypress.

INDEX